W9-AYF-371

CULTURES OF THE WORLD
Malta

Cavendish
Square
New York

Published in 2020 by Cavendish Square Publishing, LLC
243 5th Avenue, Suite 136, New York, NY 10016
Copyright © 2020 by Cavendish Square Publishing, LLC

Third Edition

Library of Congress Cataloging-in-Publication Data

Names: Sheehan, Sean, 1951- author. | Lin, Yong Jui, author. | Nevins, Debbie, author.
Title: Malta / Sean Sheehan, Yong Jui Lin, and Debbie Nevins.
Description: Third edition. | New York : Cavendish Square, [2019] | Includes bibliographical references and index. | Audience: Grades 6+
Identifiers: LCCN 2019008220 (print) | LCCN 2019008280 (ebook) | ISBN 9781502647498 (ebook) | ISBN 9781502647481 (library bound)
Subjects: LCSH: Malta--Juvenile literature. | Malta--Social life and customs--Juvenile literature.
Classification: LCC DG989.7 (ebook) | LCC DG989.7 .S54 2019 (print) | DDC 945.8/5--dc23
LC record available at https://lccn.loc.gov/2019008220

Writers, Sean Sheehan and Yong Jui Lin; Debbie Nevins, third edition
Editorial Director, third edition: David McNamara
Editor, third edition: Debbie Nevins
Art Director, third edition: Alan Sliwinski
Designer, third edition: Jessica Nevins
Production Manager, third edition: Karol Szymczuk
Cover Picture Researcher: Alan Sliwinski
Picture Researcher, third edition: Jessica Nevins

CONTENTS

MALTA TODAY

MALTA IS A SMALL ARCHIPELAGO NATION IN THE CENTER OF
the Mediterranean Sea. It's made up of two main islands, Malta and Gozo,
and a few uninhabited outcroppings. Showing up as a tiny dot on a world
map, it might seem to be of little importance, but looks can be deceiving. Malta has
played vital roles from biblical times to the modern era. Its megalithic temples bear
testimony to more than six thousand years of human history, beginning with the
arrival of unknown prehistoric sailors from neighboring lands. Empires have since
come and gone, leaving the island nation with a wealth of cultural heritage.

European and Arabic/North African traits show up in the faces and names, in
the architecture, on the dinner plate, and most noticeably, in the language. Malta's
two official languages, English and the more deeply rooted Arabic-inflected Maltese,
bear no resemblance to each other and came to the islands at very different times.
Yet most of the bilingual residents are comfortable in either tongue. Though no one
speaks Maltese outside of Malta—that is, except for the many expats living in other
parts of the world—it's Malta's English that gives it an international advantage in
business and tourism.

Long ruled by larger, more powerful nations, Malta now enjoys independence. Today the former British colony is a democratic country with a European-style parliamentary government. Although it lies midway between continental Europe and Africa, the country is geographically, politically, and culturally a part of Europe.

As such, it has been a member of the European Union (EU) since 2003, though at the time, the Maltese public was quite divided about joining. Membership in the EU provides Malta with a number of economic benefits, but it also requires the nation to meet standards in human rights, business operations, and environmental stewardship, among other things.

Prime Minister Edward Fenech Adami (*left*) and Foreign Minister Joseph Borg of Malta sign the treaty to join the European Union on April 16, 2003, in Athens, Greece.

Malta is still struggling to align with certain EU regulations, which causes problems when the Maltese people disagree with those rules. One example of this can be seen in the EU's oldest piece of environmental legislation, the Birds Directive. Written in 1979 and amended in 2009, this regulation protects the five hundred wild bird species that live in EU countries. Of those, about one-third of the species are threatened or endangered. The directive provides guidelines against the deliberate killing, capture, or trade of these species—and this is where EU law runs smack up against beloved Maltese custom. Indiscriminate bird hunting is a deeply-ingrained Maltese tradition, and some sportsmen there have no intention of following imported, imposed rules.

That's just one example of what happens when there is a clash of ideals and values between the big and the small. In this case, the European Union is the huge entity of twenty-eight nations versus the small nation of Malta. In fact, Malta is the smallest nation in the EU, in terms of both area and population.

In another clash of powers, a beloved geological rock formation on the coast of Gozo called the Azure Window met its fate on March 8, 2017. One of Malta's leading tourist attractions, the 92-foot- (28-meter-) tall natural limestone arch collapsed into stormy seas, leaving no trace of its formerly glorious self behind. The arch framed the turquoise waters of the Mediterranean that splashed at its foundations, creating a "window" of blue sea and sky scenery—and hence, the name. Although the Window looked impermeable, the forces of nature finally prevailed. The arch's death was possibly hastened by human interference, though it undoubtedly would have fallen in any case.

Despite warning signs advising—and then banning—people from walking across the formation's bridgelike top, people did so all the time. Many YouTube videos show daredevils cliff diving from the top of the formation, often

Before it collapsed in 2017, tourists often walked atop Malta's famous Azure Window.

This aerial view of Valletta, in the background, shows its densely packed buildings.

dislodging rocks along the way. In addition, there was evidence of explosives and other rock cutting techniques being employed to try to widen the arch opening, most likely to allow larger boats to sail beneath it. The Azure Window's otherworldly appearance made it a film star as well as a tourist must-see. It can be seen in several films, including *Clash of the Titans* (1981) and *The Count of Monte Cristo* (2002). The first season of the HBO series *Game of Thrones* was filmed in various locations on Malta, including at the Azure Window.

Powers of a different sort are behind some of the other problems facing Malta. As the tiny but densely populated country has boomed in recent decades, it has become a center for international banking and finance. Money equals power, and not infrequently, it also leads to corruption, and the three forces inevitably become entwined in government. Allegations of exactly that have sullied the reputation of the little island nation.

One controversial journalist was unafraid of diving into the alleged muck and broadcast her findings to her fellow citizens in her online blog, *Running Commentary*. On October 16, 2017, shortly after posting the ominous message,

"There are crooks everywhere you look now. The situation is desperate," Daphne Caruana Galizia was assassinated by a car bomb.

The news rocked Malta. The journalist's fans and critics—there are plenty of both in Malta—agreed: things like this just don't happen in Malta! Although three men were eventually charged with her murder, the consensus seemed to be that they were merely hitmen. The powerful people who hired them—and there are many possibilities—have not been identified. No one expects that they will be.

Galizia's murder caused international outrage, and the little dot on a world map that is Malta once again loomed large. Freedom of the press is considered a sign of a healthy society. In 2018, Malta's rating on the annual World Press Freedom Index fell eighteen points—the sharpest drop of all 180 countries evaluated by the group Reporters Without Borders. What does this disturbing event, along with other growing suspicions and fears, indicate about Malta's political health? The EU is concerned, to say the least, as are many Maltese themselves.

Malta cannot afford to have the shadow of corruption darkening its sunny shores. For one important thing, tourism to the islands has been growing tremendously. A reputation for catering to the world's unscrupulous, criminal elements could trigger a backlash against the country.

GEOGRAPHY

More than sixty species of plants adorn the exotic gardens of the Palazzo Parisio in Naxxar.

1

P ART WAY BETWEEN THE COASTS OF Sicily and North Africa lies the small island nation of Malta. It's made up of three main islands—the largest being Malta itself. The island of Gozo is smaller, and tiny Comino lies between the other two. Three uninhabited rocky outposts, Cominotto, Filfla, and Saint Paul's Islands, make up the rest of the Maltese archipelago.

Malta is a part of Europe, even though it lies farther south than the northernmost part of Africa. Malta is not Europe's southernmost point, however. That distinction belongs to the Greek island of Gavdos.

This aerial view of Malta shows Ċirkewwa (Marfa Point) on the island of Malta, the small island of Comino, and in the top left corner, the tip of Gozo.

Malta sits in the center of the Mediterranean Sea, which separates Europe and Africa. Fifty-eight miles (93 kilometers) to the north of Malta is the much larger island of Sicily, an autonomous region of Italy. Lying 220 miles (354 km) to the south of Malta is Tripoli, the capital of Libya, a country on Africa's northern coast. From east to west, Malta lies midway between Lebanon, a country at the eastern end of the Mediterranean, and Gibraltar at the sea's westernmost point. Gibraltar is a tiny British territory on the southern tip of Spain.

Malta's largest island is 17 miles (27 km) long and 9 miles (14 km) wide and covers an area of 95 square miles (246 square kilometers). Gozo is only 9 miles (14 km) long by 5 miles (8 km) wide, with an area of 26 square miles (67 sq km), while Comino has an area of only 1 square mile (2.6 sq km). Together, the islands cover an area of 122 square miles (316 sq km). A channel of water 3 miles (5 km) wide separates Malta and Gozo, and Comino lies between them.

This map of Malta includes the country's major cities.

TERRAIN

The three main islands are mostly composed of limestone. They rise to a maximum height of just over 829 feet (253 meters) at the Dingli Cliffs on the southwest of Malta Island. However, the land is not as flat as this might suggest. There are lots of escarpments, or steep slopes at the edge of an area of level ground that drop into a narrow valley.

One of the most prominent escarpments is the Mdina-Verdala Ridge in the Dingli Cliffs. To the north of the ridge, separated by small hills, is an array of narrow valleys that make their way down to the coast. These lower-lying areas have good alluvial soils and are cultivated with the help of irrigation.

Filfla is a small, barren, uninhabited islet located 3.1 miles (5 km) in the Mediterranean Sea south of Malta. It marks the most southerly point of the Maltese archipelago. Next

to Filfla, there is a much smaller rocky islet called Filfoletta. Filfla is about 15 acres (6 hectares) in area. It is a crumbling, flat-topped limestone plateau surrounded by 197-foot- (60 m) high cliffs.

In 1343, a chapel was built inside a cave on the islet, but it was destroyed in 1856 by an earthquake that also sank part of the island. Until 1971, the Royal Navy and Royal Air Force used the island for target practice. In 1980, it became a bird sanctuary. Three species of sea birds breed on the islet—the European storm petrel, Cory's shearwater, and yellow-legged gull. A type of wall lizard and a kind of door snail are endemic to Filfla. A large wild leek, growing up to 6.6 feet (2 m) high, also grows there.

The Filfla Natural Reserve Act, enacted in 1988, provided for further restrictions on access and use, including a prohibition on fishing within 1 nautical mile (1.9 km) around the island due to the possibility of encountering unexploded ordnance. Access to Filfla is only possible for educational or scientific purposes, and visitors must get prior permission from the ministry responsible for the environment.

Malta's terrain is mostly rocky and sparse, devoid of mountains and rivers and with little vegetation, although there are many small fields enclosed by stone walls. Between February and March, Malta is briefly transformed into myriads of colors when tulips, crocuses, and other flowers brighten up the otherwise barren countryside. The island of Gozo, thanks to the high clay content of its soil, has a more verdant landscape.

Along the coastlines are countless small harbors, creeks, bays, and sandy coves. The Grand Harbour in Valletta is a natural deepwater harbor 80 feet (24 m) deep. It has been of great economic as well as strategic importance for thousands of years. The total circumference of the shoreline around Malta Island is 84 miles (135 km), and Gozo is 27 miles (43 km) around.

FAUNA AND FLORA

Malta does not have a great variety of wildlife. The shortage of water, combined with the poor quality of the soil, has resulted in the Mediterranean shrub being the only natural vegetation. The mammals that are able to survive are mostly small animals, such as hedgehogs, weasels, and shrews. Resident birds include the Manx and Cory's shearwaters, the blue rock thrush, and the Sardinian warbler. During spring and fall, Malta is visited by countless thousands of migrating birds, but the locals enjoy shooting these birds as a popular leisure activity.

Maltese hedgehogs are protected animals. A baby like this one is called a hoglet.

Malta has no rivers. In the past, this meant complete dependence on water from wells. Small, privately owned windmills are a common sight in the countryside, where they are used to power wells to irrigate farmland. The government has built many reservoirs, and there are also a number of desalination plants, which extract salt from seawater before it is pumped into a reservoir. Desalination plants account for over 60 percent of the water used on the island, and although expensive, they have relieved the shortage of freshwater.

An old well at Misrah Mesquita Square in Mdina

Water is also pumped up from natural underground hollows in the rock where rainwater collects after percolating through the soil. Malta depends on underground reserves of freshwater. The Ta' Kandja galleries, a system of water tunnels, pump potable water to the villages. The tunnels, built in the 1950s–1960s, lie about 318 feet (97 m) below the surface and extend out under the island like the spokes of a wheel.

The Judas tree (*Cercis siliquastrum*) is common. It gets its name from the legend that it was the kind of tree from which Judas Iscariot, an apostle of Jesus Christ, hanged himself after betraying Jesus. At one time, oak trees covered the islands, but most have long since been cut down. Only a few small pockets of these indigenous trees remain.

What has survived in more plentiful numbers is the carob (*Ceratonia siliqua*), also known as the locust tree. The pods are edible, and although now mainly

used to feed cattle, they were once a source of food for hungry peasants. The juice from the pods was also used to make drinks and syrups. Other trees that are able to survive Malta's hot and dry climate include the fig, the sweet bay, and the almond.

Date palms, imported from North Africa, are a common sight. Also found in Malta are orange trees, which were also introduced to the islands.

CLIMATE

Summers in Malta are long, hot, and dry. Winters are mild, and snowfall is unknown. Although the average yearly rainfall is 24 inches (61 centimeters), it rarely rains during the summer months. The average temperature between April and October is 79.2 degrees Fahrenheit (26.2 degrees Celsius), although temperatures may rise to 96°F (36°C). In the winter months, from November to March, the average temperature is 62.2°F (16.8°C).

This typical Mediterranean combination of a long and hot summer with a dry and mild winter is ideal for attracting tourists from colder climates. Not surprisingly, Malta is very popular with visitors year-round. Moreover, because no place in Malta is more than a few miles from the sea, sea breezes help moderate the heat of the summer months. The best known of these cooling winds is the gregale (grey-GAH-lay), which blows in from high altitudes in southern Italy and Sicily. The gregale can last up to three days and is feared by fishermen because of its ability to whip up waves and endanger small craft.

In early summer and again at the end of the summer, a warm and sultry wind blows in from the Sahara Desert in Africa. Some people believe the wind, called the sirocco (*xlokk* in Maltese), affects their temperament, causing them to become annoyed by small matters that would not normally bother them. Some folks get headaches or insomnia. The warm, dry air picks up moisture as it blows across the sea, and can deliver hot, humid weather to Malta and Southern Europe. Occasionally the winds kick up into gale-force storms.

Carob bean pods hang from a carob tree, which in Maltese is called a harruba tree.

The city of Valletta shines in the Mediterranean sunlight.

URBAN CENTERS

Valletta is the capital of Malta, but it's not the largest town. The city proper has a population of 6,444. The towns of Birkirkara and Qormi have more than three times that number of people. Some 16,850 people live in Sliema, a prosperous middle-class district on Malta island. Sliema, situated close to Valletta, is home to the fashionable Tower Road, where boutiques and other upscale shops adjoin blocks of luxurious apartments.

The original capital of Malta was Mdina (m-DEE-na), an inland town. The site of this fortified city was well chosen—a high precipice on a ridge that was easy to defend. But when the Knights of Saint John arrived in the sixteenth century, they preferred a base closer to the coast. When the Great Siege of 1565 ended, the Knights committed themselves to making Malta their permanent home and built a new capital that could hold a commanding position over the main harbor. The capital was named after the leader of the Knights, the Grand Master

Since 1975, the United Nations Educational, Scientific and Cultural Organization (UNESCO) has maintained a list of international landmarks or regions considered to be of "outstanding value" to the people of the world. Such sites embody the common natural and cultural heritage of humanity, and therefore deserve particular protection. The organization works with the host country to establish plans for managing and conserving their sites. UNESCO also reports on sites which are in imminent or potential danger of destruction and can offer emergency funds to try to save the property.

The organization is continually assessing new sites to inclusion on the World Heritage list. In order to be selected, a site must be of "outstanding universal value" and meet at least one of ten criteria. These required elements include cultural value—that is, artistic, religious, or historical significance—and natural value, including exceptional beauty, unusual natural phenomena, or scientific importance.

As of January 2019, there were 1,092 sites listed, including 845 cultural, 209 natural, and 38 mixed properties in 167 nations. Of those, 54 are listed as "in danger." In Malta, three cultural sites are on the main list, and none are in danger. Malta's World Heritage Sites are the city of Valletta, "one of the most concentrated historic areas in the world"; the Ħal Saflieni Hypogeum, an enormous subterranean prehistoric structure; and the Megalithic Temples of Malta, a group of six prehistoric monuments on two islands.

Ħaġar Qim (ca. 3600–3200 BCE) is one of the Megalithic Temples of Malta.

Jean Parisot de la Valette, who had led them to their great victory over the Turks.

The largest town in Gozo is Victoria. Its original name, and one by which it is sometimes still identified, is Rabat (meaning "the town"), but this was changed by the British in 1897 in honor of Queen Victoria. Unlike the citizens of many other countries colonized by the British, the Maltese have not felt the need to assert their independence by removing linguistic markers of imperial rule.

The Rotunda of the Church of Saint John the Baptist, locally known as the Xewkija Rotunda, can be seen from the nearby city of Victoria.

INTERNET LINKS

https://www.huffpost.com/entry/secret-malta_n_4964709
"Nineteen Surprising Facts About Malta" is largely geographic in nature and includes photos for each fact.

http://staff.um.edu.mt/csav1/srg/intro_geog.pdf
This report provides basic geographic information about Malta.

https://www.telegraph.co.uk/travel/untapped-destinations/wildlife-in-malta
A British naturalist describes Maltese wildlife.

https://whc.unesco.org/en/statesparties/mt
Malta's World Heritage Site page includes links to its three listed sites.

HISTORY

The entrance to the ancient megalithic temple Ħaġar Qim is a dramatic sight.

2

FOR SUCH A SMALL, REMOTE PLACE, Malta has played a surprisingly important role in history. And history in Malta goes back a very long way. Some of the ancient megaliths found there date to the dawn of European civilization. More generally, the history of Malta can be seen to encapsulate European history as a whole. It began with the first arrival of nomadic peoples from Sicily in the north some seven thousand years ago.

The Neolithic cave-dwellers who built the megaliths were followed by a Bronze Age society. Then came a succession of rule by more powerful cultures—Carthaginians, Romans, Arabs, Normans, the Knights of Saint John, the French, and then the British at the turn of the nineteenth century. Finally, the Maltese gained their independence in 1964.

TEMPLE BUILDERS

The earliest inhabitants were Stone Age people who first arrived in Malta around 5000 BCE, probably from Sicily. Although they lacked knowledge of metals, they used their expertise with stone to leave a permanent reminder of their presence on Malta. Even before the Egyptians first began building pyramids, the Neolithic Maltese began constructing impressive

Another World Heritage Site, the Hypogeum of Ħal Saflieni in Paola, is a subterranean structure built by the same civilization that produced the Megalithic Temples. Hypogeum, *from the Greek, means "underground." This site was used as a necropolis, or burial grounds, and is made up of three levels of various chambers excavated out of the subsurface limestone. In it, archaeologists have found the remains of more than seven thousand people. The entire construction—like the temples—was accomplished using only stone and bone tools and without metal implements of any sort.*

Of the many artifacts found in the Hypogeum, the most extraordinary is a clay figure of a woman lying on a bed. Like other corpulent figures found from this era, the woman's body swells to an unnaturally full shape, and might represent fertility. The sculpture, called the Sleeping Lady, is now housed at the National Museum of Archaeology in Valletta.

The Hypogeum has been open to the public since 1908, and the many thousands of visitors affected the otherwise well preserved site. In 1990, the site was closed to the public for ten years while conservationists implemented environmental temperature and humidity controls. They also instituted a new system limiting the numbers of visitors at any given time. The site is overseen by Heritage Malta, the country's national agency for museums, conservation practice, and cultural heritage.

megalithic temples on Gozo and Malta. This great sweep of time, from 3600 to 2500 BCE, is the Temple Period of Maltese archaeology.

Some of the most famous temples dating from this period, such as the Tarxien (tar-SHEEN) temple and the Hypogeum of Ħal Saflieni, were only discovered by accident in the early twentieth century. Tarxien was uncovered when a farmer plowing his field kept blunting his plow on large stones just under the soil. Later, excavations revealed a temple complex and important prehistoric works of art. The Hypogeum, a vast underground chamber cut from rock and later used as a burial chamber, was discovered by a builder working on the foundations for a house he was building.

The era of the temple builders lasted until about 2500 BCE, at which point the civilization seems to have vanished. There is much speculation about what might have happened and whether they were completely wiped out or assimilated into a conquering culture.

PHOENICIANS AND CARTHAGINIANS

The influence of the Phoenicians and the Carthaginians was felt from around 1500 BCE to 216 BCE. The Phoenicians, a Bronze Age maritime power based in what is now Lebanon, used Malta as a staging post as they sailed from one end of the Mediterranean to the other. They also established a colony at Carthage, in what is now Tunisia in North Africa. The Carthaginians developed their own power base after Phoenicia declined in importance.

A small number of Phoenician inscriptions have been found in Malta. Being a Semitic language, it is possible that the Maltese language is Phoenician in origin, though other theories also exist. The Carthaginians also used Malta as a base, and although there is little archaeological evidence of their presence, their influence lives on in the popular Maltese name Nibblu, which is a shortened form of Hannibal, the most famous Carthaginian in history. After a fierce struggle against the power of Rome, Carthage was finally destroyed. For Malta, this heralded a long period of rule under the Romans.

THE ROMANS

Rome, which held undisputed power over the entire Mediterranean region, paid little attention to Malta even though the islands were under Roman influence for some eight hundred years. The Romans first arrived during the Second Punic War (218—201 BCE) between Rome and Carthage, and Malta fell under the responsibility of the Roman governor of Sicily.

In 60 CE, a ship heading for Rome was shipwrecked off the coast of Malta. There were well over two hundred passengers on board. One of them, Saint Paul, remained on the island for three months and converted the Roman governor, Publius. This is how Christianity came to Malta, which was one of the earliest Roman colonies to be Christianized. Today, the annual celebration of Paul's shipwreck is still an important event. If the tradition is true, then the Maltese were one of the first non-Jewish people to convert to the new religion.

THE ARABS

The islands of Malta were conquered by the Arabs in 870 CE. The new invaders retained control until the arrival of the Normans 220 years later. Not a great deal is known about how Malta was governed during this period because the conquerors regarded these small islands as only a tiny part of a vast area of influence that spread from Spain in the west, across the Mediterranean and including Sicily, to the Indus River in the east.

Malta, as in the days of Roman rule, was only a province of Sicily. Nevertheless, the short period of Arab conquest had a lasting effect on the language that developed into the Maltese that is spoken today. The introduction of citrus fruits and cotton to Malta is also attributed to the Arabs. The Arabs built their fortified capital, which they named Mdina, on the site of the old Roman capital.

Although they introduced their language to the islanders, they did not convert the people to Islam, and so Christianity retained its influence over the lives of the people of Malta.

THE NORMANS

The Normans, a group of Viking descendents from Normandy in France, conquered large parts of the Mediterranean in the eleventh century, including Sicily. In 1090, they arrived from Sicily and began to displace the Arabs as rulers of Malta. The Arabs living on Malta did not resist the Normans by force, and Muslims continued to live there as they had done before. It was not until 1224 that the Muslims were expelled from the islands.

THE KNIGHTS OF SAINT JOHN

The Order of Saint John was first established in the late eleventh century as the Hospitallers. They were a group of monks who provided medical care for Christian pilgrims traveling to the Holy Land (Jerusalem). However, the Holy Land is also holy to Islam. The pilgrims came into conflict with Arabs and therefore needed military protection. In this way, the Hospitallers evolved into an order of Christian knights drawn from the aristocratic families of Europe. They were committed to vows of celibacy, poverty, and obedience to their grand master.

As Islam grew more powerful, its followers expelled the Knights of Saint John from the Holy Land. The Knights then established a base on the island of Rhodes, off the coast of Greece. From there they could sail out to attack the enemy.

The Knights became pirates in their own way, taking every opportunity to attack Turkish merchants and rob their ships. The advance of Islam, driven by the Ottoman Empire, led to the expulsion of the Knights from Rhodes. After eight years of wandering around Europe seeking a home, they were granted the island of Malta in 1530.

The grand master, the most important rank in the order, was the official head of the Knights. The Knights adopted the distinctive eight-pointed cross, known as the Maltese Cross, as their emblem. Each of the eight points of the cross represents one of the beatitudes given in Christ's Sermon on the Mount, while the four main sections represent the Christian virtues of fortitude, justice, temperance, and prudence.

Unlike the Romans, the Norman rulers who governed Malta failed to solve the major problem of marauding pirates from North Africa. Known as corsairs, the pirates found Malta to be a useful watering hole and base for mounting attacks on passing shipping. As a result, Malta never endeared itself to the European powers, especially after a raid in 1525 that led to the capture of

Modern-day Knights of Saint John stage a historical reenactment at Fort Saint Angelo in Birgu, Malta. The man in the foreground portrays the grand bailiff of the order.

four hundred people. They were either enslaved or held for ransom. By this time, Malta had passed into the hands of the Spanish emperor, Charles V. He offered it to the Knights of Saint John, who were looking for a new home.

THE KNIGHTS TAKE MALTA

The year 1530 is very significant in Malta's history because this was when the Knights of the Order of Saint John first arrived on the islands. The Christian order exercised political and economic control over the islands. The police, the legal system, and even the water supply were all controlled by the order, and all the key positions in the administration of Malta were held by Knights. The local population, which numbered around twelve thousand in 1530, had little contact with the Knights, but they were subject to them. Thanks to the order's control of the police and military garrisons, the population had little choice but to accept their authority.

THE GREAT SIEGE

The Knights found the inland capital of Mdina to be inconvenient, so they set about building new bases on the coast. In May 1565, the Ottoman Empire invaded the island of Malta. A huge fleet of Turkish ships with forty thousand men arrived, aiming to completely destroy the Knights. It took them a month to take Fort Saint Elmo, but the Knights in Fort Saint Angelo managed to hold out against a total surrender of the island. In September, when Christian reinforcements began to arrive, the Turks sailed away and the Great Siege was over. The Great Siege has entered Maltese history as one of the nation's great defining moments. The Knights' grand master, Jean Parisot de la Valette, survived the siege with just six hundred men, while the leader of the Ottomans, Dragut, died in the fighting.

AFTER THE SIEGE

The Knights were determined to secure their island home against any future attack, so work soon began on the building of Valletta. The town took five years to complete, gave the Knights a secure home for more than two hundred years, and heralded an age of prosperity for Malta. By the mid-eighteenth century, however, the Turkish Ottoman Empire was in decline and no longer posed a threat. The rule of the Knights came to an end in 1798. Napoleon Bonaparte of France captured Malta and confiscated all their land and property. The revolutionary and anticlerical French army also abolished the Maltese nobility.

But by attacking the Catholic Church, the French made many enemies. When Napoleon set off for Egypt, he left only a small force behind. When the Maltese rose in rebellion, the French were taken by surprise. They managed to hold out in Valletta until 1800 but finally surrendered. Malta fell into the hands of France's enemy at the time, the British.

BRITISH RULE

At first, the British did not realize the strategic importance of their new acquisition. But in time they came to appreciate the usefulness of a small group of islands in the middle of the Mediterranean. This became even more evident after the opening of the Suez Canal in Egypt in 1869.

But all was not well on those islands. After World War I (1914—1918), the Maltese people staged popular demonstrations calling for more say in the running of their country. During one demonstration in 1919, British troops shot four people dead. Later the same year, the British announced plans to

Domenico (Dom) Mintoff was born in 1916 into a poor family. At the time, Malta was just one of Britain's many overseas territories, and it had very little control over its own affairs. Mintoff trained as a civil engineer but became more interested in politics. He helped organize the Labour Party's first electoral victory in 1947 before going on to become the leader of the party. He was prime minister four times before finally stepping down in 1984.

Mintoff became the best-known Maltese politician internationally, mainly due to his relationship with Britain. At one point, Mintoff was so pro-British that he suggested Malta should become an integral part of the United Kingdom itself. When this was rejected by Britain, his own position changed, and he later led the demands for full independence.

Mintoff is equally famous for his battles with the Catholic Church in Malta. He dared to openly criticize the church for its authoritarianism and for its great wealth. He attempted to confiscate church property and limit the political influence of priests. As a socialist, he struggled to improve the quality of life for the ordinary citizens of Malta, and in this respect, he achieved a great deal. Many important improvements, such as the introduction of free higher education, were due to his efforts. Though he died in 2012, he is still revered by many Maltese.

draw up a more liberal constitution. The new constitution kept power over important matters such as defense and immigration in the hands of the British. However, it also created a Maltese government with an elected assembly to govern many other aspects of life.

This system worked well until 1933, when the British suspended the Maltese government. The British disapproved of Maltese attempts to reintroduce Italian as the language of instruction in schools instead of English. Before the arrival of the British, the official language since 1530 (and the language of the educated elite) had been Italian, but this was downgraded by the increased use of English. In 1934, English and Maltese were declared the sole official languages. For the next fourteen years, the Maltese government remained suspended.

WORLD WAR II

The strategic importance of Malta in any struggle for control of the Mediterranean became obvious during World War II. Several German generals called for an invasion of the island nation because as long as it remained in British hands, enemy planes and submarines would be able to use it as a base. This would allow the British to attack the German convoys that were supplying their troops in the war in North Africa.

Adolf Hitler, however, preferred to launch an aerial attack. He planned to bomb and starve Malta into submission by subjecting it to a second great siege. The island became one of the most heavily bombed targets during World War II. In two months in 1942, for example, more bombs were dropped on Malta than on all of London in a year. Many families moved to Gozo, where there was only a single small runway to attract the attention of enemy planes.

As essential supplies dwindled, it seemed almost certain that Malta would be forced to surrender. Everything came to depend on an Allied convoy of

Two hundred years after their expulsion from Malta by Napoleon's troops, the Knights of Saint John made a triumphant return when they were granted a ninety-nine-year lease on Fort Saint Angelo in 1998. The fort was the scene of their greatest victory in 1565, when some six hundred Knights and eight thousand Maltese soldiers stemmed the tide of Muslim expansionism by successfully holding out against forty thousand Turks and their armada of three hundred ships.

Today, the order is known as the Sovereign Military Hospitaller Order of Saint John of Jerusalem, of Rhodes, and of Malta. It is also called the Sovereign Military Order of Malta (SMOM), the Order of Malta, or the Knights of Malta for short. It is a Roman Catholic order based in Rome, Italy, and a sovereign subject of international law. The order currently has 13,500 members, along with many thousands of volunteers and medical personnel, including doctors, nurses, auxiliaries, and paramedics. Their goal is to assist the elderly, the handicapped, refugees, children, the homeless, and those with terminal illnesses and leprosy in five continents of the world, without distinction of race or religion. Through its worldwide relief corps, Malteser International, the order also aids victims of natural disasters, epidemics, and armed conflicts.

fourteen supply ships. Escorted by battleships, aircraft carriers, cruisers, and destroyers, it set out on a final rescue mission in 1942. The convoy was an easy target for enemy planes and submarines, and the attempt to reach Malta became a dramatic journey through a corridor of bombs and torpedoes. When the SS *Ohio*, the first of the five supply ships that survived, was finally towed into Grand Harbour, it was met by cheering crowds and tears of relief.

INDEPENDENCE

In the first general election after World War II, Malta got its first Labour government. In 1955, Dominic Mintoff became the leader of the Labour Party. A charismatic and controversial politician, Mintoff led Malta's demands for full independence from Britain, which was finally achieved in 1964. The main difficulties facing the country were economic, a major setback being Britain's decision to cut its own defense budget by abandoning expensive overseas bases. In Malta, where the British employed about one in five of Malta's working population in the British-owned local dockyards, this forced the country to look to its own future.

In 1979, the British military base in Malta was finally closed, and the last of the British forces sailed away from the islands for the last time. Malta was now truly independent and entirely responsible for its own affairs.

In the same year, the first overtures were made to the European Economic Community (now the European Union, or EU), and in 1990 a formal application to join the EU was submitted. In a 2003 referendum on EU membership, a majority of Malta's voters were in favor of membership. Malta joined the EU on May 1, 2004, and on January 1, 2008, it adopted the euro, the currency of the EU.

INTERNET LINKS

https://artsandculture.google.com/exhibit/bgKS7KPNk-UDKw
The Sleeping Lady of Ħal Saflieni is the subject of this annotated slide show.

https://www.maltauncovered.com/malta-history
This site offers a brief overview and a detailed timeline of Malta's history.

https://www.malteser-international.org/home.html
Maltese International details its work in many needy countries.

https://www.orderofmalta.int
The website of the Sovereign Order of Malta provides information on the group's present-day mission and activities.

https://www.theguardian.com/world/2012/aug/21/dom-mintoff
This obituary for Dom Mintoff tells the story of his life and accomplishments.

GOVERNMENT

The Independence Monument in Floriana was erected to commemorate the twenty-fifth anniversary of Malta's independence from the United Kingdom.

MALTA BECAME AN INDEPENDENT state on September 21, 1964, adopting a system of parliamentary democracy based on regular elections and universal suffrage. Until December 13, 1974, when the country became a republic, Malta still recognized the British monarch, and a governor-general representing the crown lived in Valletta.

Today the head of state is the president. Although the president appoints the prime minister and the leader of the opposition, he or she does not hold political power. Executive power rests with the prime minister, who chooses a cabinet of ministers to govern the country.

Malta remains a member of the Commonwealth, which is an international association of the United Kingdom and countries that were once part of the British Empire. The British monarch is the symbolic head of the Commonwealth.

THE CONSTITUTION

The constitution of Malta in use today is the same one that was established in 1964 upon achieving independence. However, it has been amended more than thirty times. In 2014, for example, the anti-discrimination provision

3

Malta's foreign policy is governed by a commitment to neutrality. The constitution does not allow the country to join a military alliance, such as NATO, or to allow foreign military bases on its territory.

The Parish Church of the Assumption, locally called the Rotunda of Mosta, is one of many landmark Catholic churches in Malta.

limited form of self-government, people continued to turn to their priests for advice. At the same time, the church was eager to ensure that its power and influence would not be eroded by support for secular politicians.

Problems arose when disagreements between the church and the Labour Party began. In the 1950s and 1960s, matters came to a head when Prime Minister Dom Mintoff confronted the political power and ambitions of the church. When the Labour Party formed the government in 1955, it tried to limit the power of the church by subjecting it to taxation and by removing the immunity of the archbishop and bishops from the authority of the criminal and civil courts.

In the 1962 election, the church told the people of Malta, who were overwhelmingly Catholic, that it would be a sin to vote for the Labour Party and that even reading a Labour Party newspaper was against God's wishes. The opposition Nationalist Party won the 1962 election and was reelected in 1966 when the church again sided with the Nationalist Party and warned people not to vote for the Labour Party.

The church is still a powerful force in Maltese politics, but it's not what it used to be. In 2017, for example, Malta legalized same-sex marriage over heavy church opposition.

INTERNET LINKS

https://www.gov.mt/en/Pages/home.aspx
This official government page offers a good overview of the Maltese government.

http://justiceservices.gov.mt/DownloadDocument.aspx?app=lom&itemid=8566
A PDF of Malta's constitution is available at this link.

https://www.npr.org/2018/07/22/630866527/mastermind-behind-malta-journalist-killing-remains-a-mystery
This is an account of the murder of Daphne Caruana Galizia and the aftermath.

https://www.theguardian.com/commentisfree/2018/oct/16/murder-justice-daphne-caruana-galizia-malta
This opinion piece by the famed author Margaret Atwood questions the investigation into Caruana Galizia's murder.

ECONOMY

MALTA HAS AN INDUSTRIALIZED, service-based, free-market economy. It's a small economy, since Malta is such a small country, but it's a strong one nonetheless. The economy is bolstered by Malta's geographic location in the middle of the Mediterranean Sea, where it's a natural crossroads between Europe, Africa, and the Middle East. In addition, its people provide a strong labor force. Most Maltese speak English and are well educated, which helps in the vital tourism and financial services sectors. In addition, the economy relies on foreign trade and manufacturing, particularly electronics and pharmaceuticals.

However, Malta does face some economic challenges. For example, the country produces less than a quarter of the food its people need, it has limited water supplies, and it has few domestic energy sources.

Malta joined the European Union in 2004 and adopted the euro as its currency on January 1, 2008. From 2014 through 2016, Malta led the eurozone in growth, expanding more than 4.5 percent per year.

4

The number of tourists who visit the islands of Malta each year is about five times the size of the country's population.

farms cannot compete globally with the huge industrial-scale farms throughout much of Europe. The number of people working full-time in agriculture had fallen to a mere 1,372 in a national survey completed in 2013, with more people working only part time in the field. Those people are also growing older, and there are fewer young people entering farming.

To combat these problems, the government is working with the EU to revitalize Malta's agricultural sector. A 2014–2020 Rural Development Program aims to increase job creation with the goal of attracting young people. The plan focuses on modernization, innovation, and more environmentally friendly practices for farmers.

Similar problems confront the fishing industry. Being a small island nation, Malta has naturally relied on fishing as a major occupation for many generations. But now the small-scale fishing tradition in Malta is dying out. The remaining fishermen are advancing in age, and not enough young people are taking up fishing to replace them. There are several reasons for this trend. Extreme overfishing in the Mediterranean has taken a huge toll on the average fisherman's take. Studies show that more than 90 percent of fishable species in that region are overfished. Meanwhile, Malta's small-scale fishers, using line-fishing technology, cannot compete in international waters with the large fishing vessels from larger nations using purse seines (a type of drag net). Tuna, swordfish, and dorado were once plentiful catches for Maltese fishermen, but no longer.

In 2017, there were only 377 full-time fishermen in Malta, of which 314 were small-scale operations. Only twenty-two long-line tuna fishers remained, and the swordfish population in the central Mediterranean had utterly collapsed.

TOURISM

Tourism is an important and growing segment of the economy, contributing about 15 percent to the GDP. In 2017, more than 2.3 million tourists visited the nation, with the peak month being August. The government's success in promoting Malta as an international business center has also contributed significantly to Malta's economy. Most tourists, however, go to Malta for vacation time. By far, most are from Great Britain, followed by Italy. The remaining tourists come mostly from other European nations, the United States, and Australia.

The Blue Lagoon on the island of Comino is a popular tourist attraction, though the island itself is essentially unpopulated.

INTERNET LINKS

https://agriculture.gov.mt/en/agric/Pages/nationalAgriPolicy.aspx
This government page includes a link to an in-depth PDF about Malta's agricultural policy for 2018—2028.

https://www.bloomberg.com/news/features/2018-09-11/why-the-eu-is-furious-with-malta
This in-depth article explores the EU's allegations of corruption in Malta.

http://www.mta.com.mt
The Malta Tourism Authority offers statistics and information about the tourism industry.

https://www.timesofmalta.com/articles/view/20171001/local/fishermen-on-the-brink.659267
This article takes a hard look at Malta's fishing industry.

ENVIRONMENT

The Blue Grotto on the southern coast of Malta is a complex of seven caves. Inside, the submerged flora glow with phosphorescent colors.

5

N 2018, THE CONSTITUTION OF MALTA was amended to include the following statement: "The State shall protect and conserve the environment and its resources for the benefit of the present and future generations and shall take measures to address any form of environmental degradation in Malta, including that of air, water and land, and any sort of pollution problem and to promote, nurture and support the right of action in favour of the environment."

The new sentence directs the government of Malta to take good care of the environment. It doesn't tell the authorities how to do it, just that it must do so. For the most part, the Maltese public agrees with the need to safeguard their country's environment. Although it's not plagued by some of the immense problems facing some other nations, Malta does have its challenges.

The European Union, of which Malta is a member, is far more specific with its directions for environmental stewardship. As in other aspects of twenty-first century Maltese life, aligning with EU policy and law is a priority.

The Maltese rock-centaury (*Cheirolophus crassifolius*) is the national plant of Malta. The purple flower, a member of the aster family, is native to the Maltese islands, where it is found on the cliffs of Wied Babu, a scenic valley in western Malta.

THE MAIN CHALLENGES

In 2017, the European Commission (EC) reported that Malta's main challenges in meeting EU environmental standards were:

- speeding up the implementation of EU waste-management requirements, as landfill rates were extremely high and recycling rates very low;

- improving water management to ensure protection of water bodies and prevent flash floods;

- improving the air quality in the most urbanized areas by introducing systemic solutions for transport congestion, and

- improving the protection of habitats and species of EU interest by fully implementing the Natura 2000 requirements ... and strengthening the enforcement of the Birds Directive.

Heavy traffic in Sliema is indicative of Malta's dense population.

CAUSES OF POLLUTION

Malta's air pollution is among the worst in Europe, and car emissions are the main culprit. The country's dense population translates into correspondingly dense traffic on the roads. In March 2018, there were 375,041 vehicles on the road—78 percent of which were passenger cars—and the number has been steadily increasing each year. Of those, 60.3 percent of the vehicles were gasoline-powered, and 39 percent had diesel engines. Only 0.5 percent were electric or hybrid vehicles, translating to a total of 1,426 alternative fuel cars on Malta's roads.

These numbers put Malta high up in its ratio of vehicles to people, as compared to other European countries. In 2016, for example, Malta averaged 615 cars per 1,000 inhabitants, which was the third-highest ratio in Europe, behind only Italy (625 cars) and Luxembourg (662 cars). The EU average that year was 505 cars per 1,000 people.

Prime Minister Joseph Muscat has said that the government would be considering setting a cut-off date beyond which all new cars would have to be electric.

Other sources of air pollution include the natural particulate matter that blows in from Africa, carrying dust from the Sahara Desert. Sea spray also carries dust, and Malta is vulnerable to this source from all sides. The Mediterranean Sea itself is significantly polluted. It has some of the highest levels of plastic pollution in the world.

ENERGY

Malta has no fossil fuel or hydroelectric resources of its own; it's completely dependent on importing energy. In 2015, Malta connected to Europe's power grid, ending the country's electrical isolation. The 59-mile- (95 k) long Malta—Sicily interconnector lies under the sea and hooks Malta into the Italian Transmission Network, which is part of the European grid. The power exchange works in both directions—the cable not only allows Malta to receive electricity but also to exchange it with the Italian power market.

Natura 2000 is a coordinated network of protected areas in Europe for the purpose of providing core breeding and resting sites for rare and threatened species. The habitats stretch across all EU countries, both on land and at sea.

That same year, Malta closed its old Marsa electric power generating station, which dated to 1953. The old oil-burning plant had been widely criticized for contributing to the country's air pollution. By 2018, the plant had been completely dismantled and demolished. The Delimara power station complex at Marsaxlokk continues to provide electricity for the nation.

The extensive use of fossil fuels in Malta for transportation, production, and electricity generation is causing health risks for the Maltese population, including lung cancer and heart disease, and the prevalence of asthma among Maltese children and young adults has steadily increased in recent years.

Until recently, Malta hadn't made much headway into instituting alternative sources of energy such as wind or solar power. With three hundred days a year of sunshine, solar certainly seemed to be an option worth exploring. But lately, Malta has jumped onto the solar bandwagon with great enthusiasm. After installing 35.3 megawatts of photovoltaic energy in just two years to reach a total of 109.2 MW, Malta had surged to fourth place in the EU by 2018, when calculated on a per capita basis. Plans are being developed to build about two dozen solar farms.

However, solar farms often require a great deal of open space, and that's something Malta doesn't have much of. The country's solar farm policy bans development in the open countryside. Old filled-in quarries and former landfills are the preferred sites for this use.

WASTE AND RECYCLING

Being a small island nation, Malta has little space for landfills and waste treatment plants. The country also has a population that tends to generate way more than the average amount of waste. In 2016, Malta ranked as the second most wasteful country in Europe, after only Denmark, in terms of the amount of waste generated per capita. That year, the figure was 1,426 pounds (647 kg) of waste per person per year. The EU average for 2016, meanwhile, was 1,058 pounds (480 kg) per person.

By 2018, it appeared that Malta might miss its 2020 municipal waste recycling target. The European Commission cited a general lack of incentives to

Litter and discarded tires contaminate a rocky seashore in Malta.

prod the public to cooperate with the recycling program as one of the reasons. Another was an insufficient number of collection centers and systems for recyclables and biowaste.

The government, for its part, stepped up its efforts. It announced the construction of a new waste-to-energy plant in Magħtab, scheduled for completion in 2023. The incinerator is planned to process 40 percent of Malta's waste, with the rest being recycled. As to that, lawmakers were considering making recycling mandatory, with noncompliance punishable by fines, to compel reluctant recyclers to clean up their act.

The Birds Directive is an EU environmental law based on the understanding that migratory birds can only be protected with cross-border cooperation. The legislation addresses habitat protection and management, hunting practices, trade, and tracking the populations of various species to ascertain their health and numbers.

CONSERVATION ORGANIZATIONS

The Environment and Resources Authority is the government regulatory agency responsible for the natural environment in Malta.

Nature Trust Malta, a partner of the World Wildlife Fund, works to protect Malta's plants and animals. It provides habitat conservation and restoration, runs educational programs, and maintains a twenty-four-hour, professionally trained animal rescue team.

Bird Life Malta is the most effective and successful organization in the fight against the illegal hunting of protected bird species in Malta. It maintains nature reserves and monitors species populations, rescues and rehabilitates injured bids, and fights wildlife crime. The organization presses for more legislative protections and uses education to change Malta's deeply ingrained bird-shooting tradition.

PLANT AND ANIMAL LIFE

The Maltese islands, although small in area (122 square miles/316 sq km), host a large number of endemic species, some of which are unique and unusual. These endemic species are important to the Maltese islands because they form part of Maltese national heritage and are topics of scientific research.

FLORA Although small compared with other countries, the Maltese islands contain many special flowers found only in Malta.

The Maltese rock-centaury is the national plant of Malta. The plant is native to the Maltese islands. It is commonly found in the limits of Wied Babu in Malta. The flower's conservation status is listed as threatened.

The Maltese everlasting is another native species of flowering plant. The rare bush grows up to 3.3 feet (1 meter) and is found only on the western cliffs of Gozo and on Fungus Rock. Its bright yellow flowers can be seen during the months of May and June. Its long and narrow whitish leaves have a covering of short hair. Its natural habitats are Mediterranean-type shrubby vegetation and rocky shores. It is threatened by habitat loss.

FAUNA There are more endemic animals than plants in the Maltese islands. Very often, these endemic Maltese animals have been confused with a similar but different species from a neighboring country.

MALTESE FRESHWATER CRAB The Maltese freshwater crab is very rare, and its numbers have been decreasing in recent years. Known as the *qabru* in Maltese, it's a decapod, a crustacean with ten legs, that can grow up to 3.1 inches (8 cm) in width. The crab is greenish-gray, with some occasional orange-yellow patches, and purplish legs. It lives where fresh or running water is present throughout the year. It is found in Mtahleb, Baħrija, and San Martin in Malta, and in the Lunzjata Valley in Gozo. The numbers of this freshwater crab are steadily declining as a result of water pollution, the drying up of streams, and hunting.

MALTESE WALL LIZARD The Filfola lizard, or Maltese wall lizard, is found in the Pelagian Islands of Italy, as well as in Malta. This lizard's natural habitats include Mediterranean-type shrubby vegetation, rocky areas, rocky shores,

A Maltese wall lizard scurries across a rock.

The rocky shore of Majjistral Nature and History Park is a part of the Natura 2000 network of protected natural habitats.

arable land, pastureland, and rural gardens. In the Maltese islands, there are four, possibly five, subspecies of the Maltese wall lizard, and all are endemic. Unlike the males, which are bright in color, young lizards and females are somewhat dull brown.

NATIONAL PARKS AND RESERVES

GHADIRA NATURE RESERVE

The Ghadira Nature Reserve occupies an area of about 14.8 acres (6 ha) and occupies the floodplain between two ridges. It is some 328 feet (100 m) from Mellieha Bay's sandy beach. More than two hundred species of birds have been spotted at the reserve, and many birds spend the winter here.

MAJJISTRAL NATURE AND HISTORY PARK Malta's first natural park is situated in the northwest of Malta, in an area dominated by coastal cliffs. Waves have eroded the clay slopes to the point where large sections of overhanging limestone have collapsed, forming the boulder scree. This has created a special habitat for plants, and due to its relative inaccessibility, it has remained an unspoiled landscape.

The erosion of the rock has also formed sandy beaches. The island's northwest region, in fact, boasts a number of beautiful bays, including Fomm ir-Rih, Jnejna, Ghajn Tuffieha, Golden Sands, and Paradise Bay. These are all surrounded by magnificent views of clay slopes, boulder scree, and cliffs.

The outstanding landscape in the park has attracted a number of hikers over the years. While visitors flock to beaches such as Golden Sands in the hot months in order to cool down, the months between October and April bring the landscape to life with the onset of the fall rains. The climate is mild and perfect for walks in the park.

Various features of cultural interest that merit conservation lie within the boundaries of the park. These features include cart ruts, stone walls, farmhouses, small beehives, tombs dating to the Classical period, natural caves, and numerous stone huts that lie within and outside the park. Of particular interest is a rare stone hut constructed in a square shape. Rural stone huts were used for both storage and shelter.

On the two sides of the valley overlooking Golden Bay, there are entrenchments built as part of a coastal defense system in the early eighteenth century, during the period of the Knights of Saint John.

INTERNET LINKS

https://birdlifemalta.org
This site provides news and information about bird protection in Malta.

http://ec.europa.eu/environment/nature/legislation/birdsdirective/index_en.htm
Information about the European Commission's Birds Directive and Natura 2000 can be found on this site.

https://era.org.mt
The site of Malta's Environment and Resources Authority offers the most recent State of the Environment report.

https://www.naturetrustmalta.org
Nature Trust Malta reports on environmental concerns with up-to-date news stories.

https://oceana.org/blog/overfishing-and-pollution-have-trashed-mediterranean
This article details the pollution of the Mediterranean Sea.

THE MALTESE

A young Maltese boy enjoys a high vantage point during a religious feast celebration in the town of Hamrun.

6

BEING A SMALL BUT DENSELY populated island nation, Malta is home to only one main ethnic group of people. Perhaps its physical isolation in the Mediterranean helps to explain why Malta is populated by such a remarkably homogeneous people. The Maltese have a strong sense of identity and national pride that binds them together. However, as the country's long history makes clear, the country has been conquered and ruled by a series of more powerful nations, and Malta has only been an independent nation since 1964.

It is not surprising, therefore, that facial features reveal a mix of influences. Although the Maltese are a highly individual people, the face of a Maltese person reflects a fairly unique fusion of the West (through the rule of ancient Rome and later European powers) and an Arab influence that goes back to the days of the Phoenicians. Genetically, the Maltese are most similar to Southern Italians.

Borg is the most popular surname in Malta, with one of every twenty-five people having this last name. Other popular surnames are Vella, Farrugia, Camilleri, Zammit, Grech, Galea, Caruana, Agius, and Cassar.

People enjoy the sunshine at an outdoor café in Valletta.

CHARACTERISTICS

Because the Maltese have been exposed for so long to other cultural influences, many national characteristics are the result of a blending of foreign cultures. To a lesser or greater degree, this is true of nearly all cultures, but it applies particularly to the Maltese. A good example is the very strong attachment to the Roman Catholic faith and its practices that is also found in Italy and especially Sicily.

An important difference, and one that goes some way to explaining what is unique about the Maltese, is Malta's internationalism. The country has been—and because of mass tourism, continues to be—remarkably open to foreign influences.

Yet, despite this, the people maintain their own dignity and way of life without feeling threatened or aggrieved in any way. The "no little kindness" that the Bible records as being afforded to Saint Paul is an aspect of Maltese hospitality, which many tourists feel is a distinguishing and highly attractive aspect of the culture. Many foreign tourists enjoy coming to the country because they feel they are treated with the same respect that the Maltese extend to their own people.

Many Maltese have a strong, almost old-fashioned, sense of dignity and manners. This may be partly because Malta is not subjected to the relentless pace of modern European society. The more relaxed lifestyle allows people to interact with others in a way that seems almost stress-free.

POPULATION

The population of Malta was 449,050 in 2018, including about 31,000 people on Gozo. This makes the country one of the world's more densely populated areas. This is especially true of the main island of Malta, where about half the total population lives in a small urban area around Valletta and the Grand

The "old town" section of Valletta is a UNESCO World Heritage Site, featuring 320 historic buildings and monuments within an area of only 136 acres (55 ha).

Harbour. One reason for this comparatively large population is because the Catholic Church has been able to discourage the use of contraception, and until recently, families tended to be large.

About 115,973 Maltese live overseas, mostly in Australia, Britain, Canada, and the United States. The population of Malta also undergoes a massive, although temporary, surge every summer when 1.2 million tourists fly in to enjoy the hospitable climate, the beaches, and the welcoming atmosphere. About half a million summer visitors come from Britain.

The British also make up the majority of the 6,500 foreign residents who live on the islands. Many of them are senior citizens who have chosen to retire in Malta.

GOZITANS

About 31,000 to 37,000 people live on the island of Gozo, and although they are Maltese, they always refer to themselves as "Gozitans." This is more an expression of their sense of pride than a wish to be independent of Malta. The people of Gozo have a sense of their own identity as islanders, but they have

The green fields of Gozo reflect the residents' rural lifestyle.

no serious political disagreement with the Maltese government, nor do they have any wish to be treated as a separate group. There are, however, some noticeable differences in outlook between the people who live on the island of Malta and those who have lived all their lives on Gozo. Gozitans are more accustomed to a rural way of life, and up until very recently, they have not benefited as much from economic progress.

NICKNAMES

Nicknames, as a familiar way of identifying certain people, are common to many cultures around the world, but in Malta they are woven into the fabric of everyday life. In rural communities, they still play a part in social life. According to sociologists, the relatively limited number of surnames available in Malta accounts for the common practice of identifying individuals by nicknames. One village, consisting of nearly 250 different households, was found to have fewer than sixty surnames, so the use of nicknames serves a practical purpose.

What is interesting about nicknames in Malta is that they can be used as a familiar term of address. This is fairly unique to Malta. In neighboring Mediterranean cultures, such as Sicily, for example, many nicknames are insults and would never be used to actually address a person. Maltese nicknames, on the other hand, are mainly harmless. For example, a man whose hobby is catching birds with a homemade trap may be known by the name of a particular species of bird.

INTERNET LINKS

https://www.um.edu.mt/think/the-hidden-history-of-the -maltese-genome
This accessible article provides an unusual look at the history of the Maltese people through genomic studies.

http://worldpopulationreview.com/countries/malta-population
This site provides demographic statistics for Malta.

LIFESTYLE

A young man sips his coffee at a tiny table outside a café in Valletta.

7

The Maltese people appear to be getting happier. In 2018, Malta was rated the 22nd happiest country on Earth. According to the World Happiness Report, issued by the UN Sustainable Development Solutions Network, Malta rose five points in the ranking, up from number 27 in 2017. And that was a three-point rise over the year before. The happiest country in 2018 was Finland, and the least happy, at number 156, was the African nation of Burundi.

LIFE ON THE ISLAND OF MALTA IS bustling and active, while life on neighboring Gozo is peaceful and slow. The only way to get from one island to the other is by boat, and many people, in Gozo at least, want to leave it that way.

In general, an unhurried pace is a central characteristic of Maltese life, and it is reflected in the people's lifestyle in various ways. The Maltese work hard, but they know how to balance their lives. They enjoy good conversation and exchanging news, and many festive events bear testimony to their capacity to enjoy life outside of work.

The Maltese lifestyle could very generally be described as a Mediterranean one, but with a particularly Maltese flavor.

THE WORKING DAY

Most working Maltese tend to rise early. Farmers and other outdoor workers often start work around 7 a.m. Office workers and employees in manufacturing plants and factories usually start work an hour later, or by 9 a.m. at the latest. By this time, shops are generally open.

Small bakeries and butchers open early in the morning, and vendors selling fresh vegetables set up in their regular locations by erecting a small table extension from the back of their small vans. Many shops close for a few hours during the hottest part of the afternoon. This afternoon rest period, the siesta, is common to most Mediterranean cultures. Nevertheless, some visitors may find it strange that so many places close

The Catholic Church still plays an important role in education, and it runs its own schools alongside state schools. Under an agreement between the church and the state of Malta, Catholic schools are free of charge. About 30 percent of all students attend non-state (both Catholic and private) schools.

Every year, well over half of students who reach the age of sixteen choose to continue their education. A variety of post-secondary courses are available, ranging from academic programs designed as pre-university courses to vocational programs in areas such as tourism, agriculture, health care, and technical education.

The University of Malta is the oldest university in the British Commonwealth outside of Britain. The university's history dates back to 1592, when the Jesuits founded the college, which became renowned for its scholarship throughout the Mediterranean. In 1768, it became a university. Today, along with its main campus in Msida, it also has campuses in Velletta, Marsaxlokk, and Gozo. Altogether, the university serves more than 11,500 students each year, including about 1,000 international students from around ninety different countries. The courses are taught in English.

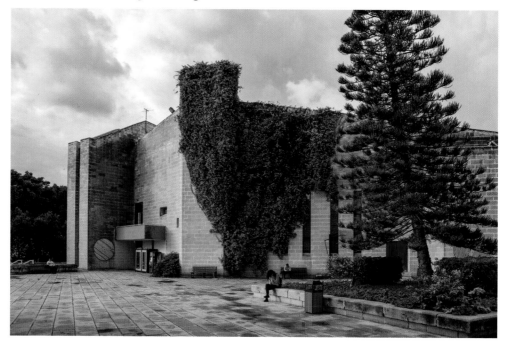

One of the buildings at the University of Malta sports the iconic "ivy-league" appearance.

BUS TRAVEL

Although many people own cars, public transportation still plays an important role in many people's lives. This is especially true for older citizens and young people who do not have their own cars. Since a 7-mile (11 km) stretch of railway was closed in 1931, the bus network has been the sole means of public transportation and has spread to encompass nearly every corner of the main island. Malta's fleet of nearly four hundred buses carries some forty-eight million passengers per year.

In the old days—not that long ago, really—Malta was known for its old-fashioned, classic buses. The vehicles became tourist attractions in their own right and were depicted on many Maltese advertisements to promote tourism, as well as on gifts and merchandise for tourists. The buses in Malta were all dark

People look at a public transportion map of Malta at the Buġibba bus station.

A traditional Maltese form of transportation, dating back to the mid-nineteenth century, is the horse-drawn carriage known as a karozzin (ca-rotts-SEEN). These vehicles hold up to four passengers on high seats, with a canopy to provide shade. They are still used by some Maltese, especially on Gozo, for short trips, such as a social visit to friends on a Sunday. Although they are occasionally used for special events such as weddings and funerals, they are mostly a tourist attraction in the cities.

Some Maltese have been calling for a ban on karozzini, claiming the work is cruel and hazardous to the horses that pull them. On a particularly hot day in August 2018, a karozzin horse dropped dead on the street in Floriana, and the country erupted in an uproar. Four days later, when the temperature reached 100°F (38°C), another working horse fainted and collapsed. Some people, backed by the organizations Animal Liberation Malta and Vegan Malta, called for a ban on karozzini. Others demanded new rules and regulations to better protect the animals. But yet other animal rights proponents pointed out that if karozzini were banned, most of the horses would likely be slaughtered, as their owners could no longer afford to keep them, and there are few options in Malta for rescued horses.

yellow, with a band of orange, while those on the sister island of Gozo were gray, with a red band. Many had amusing or creative customized modification and decorations.

However, most of the vintage buses were phased out in 2011 due to environmental concerns. A new fleet of modern buses has been introduced. After several years of problematic private management, the bus network was nationalized in 2014 as Malta Public Transport. One year later, the service was reprivatized, but it kept the same name.

Colorful old buses from the 1960s were once used as public transport in Malta.

The organization Heritage Malta, which oversees many of the nation's historic sites, purchased ninety of the older buses after the restructuring of the bus network. Their aim was to restore them to their original condition for the sake of preserving the country's heritage. Some are run as independent businesses for weddings and special occasions.

INTERNET LINKS

https://www.gov.uk/guidance/living-in-malta
A significant number of British people move to Malta, so this UK government page offers guidance and information.

https://lovinmalta.com/lifestyle/living-in-malta
This Maltese media site offers many articles relating to lifestyle.

https://www.um.edu.mt
This is the site of the University of Malta.

RELIGION

The 1658 painting *Saint George on Horseback* by Mattia Preti dominates the altar of the Chapel of the Langue of Aragon in Saint John's Co-cathedral in Valletta.

8

MALTA IS STRONGLY AND predominantly Roman Catholic, yet its Catholicism has qualities unlike those of other Catholic countries. This is evident in the multitude of festivals that take place every year, for although they nearly all have a religious origin, they are regarded by many Maltese as festive, social events.

Like many other European countries, Malta has changed with the times. The Roman Catholic Church no longer wields the enormous power it once had over people's daily lives. Besides Catholicism, there are several other religious groups in Malta, including Anglicans, Methodists, Greek Orthodox, Jews, Muslims, and some small evangelical groups. Under the country's constitution, however, Roman Catholicism is the state religion and must be taught in state schools.

CHRISTIANITY

According to legend, Christianity came to Malta with one of Christ's disciples, Saint Paul, who was shipwrecked on the island. At the time, Malta was occupied by the Romans, and Saint Paul was brought to the capital and allowed to preach Christianity. The Roman governor, Publius, and his family were converted, and he ordered that Christianity become the religion of the country. In this way, Malta became one of the first countries in the world to adopt Christianity.

In 2011, Malta became one of the last countries in the world to legalize divorce. Voters approved a referendum on the proposal by only 53 percent after a bitter campaign. The Catholic Church in Malta aggressively fought against the proposition. Following this move, only the Philippines and Vatican City now forbid divorce.

The period of Arab domination interrupted Christian rule, but it was resumed with the arrival of the Normans, who reestablished the religion on an official basis. In 1530, the Knights of the Order of Saint John arrived on the island, giving new power to the religion's hold over the people. After a very short period of anticlerical French rule under Napoleon, the church reestablished its power during the nineteenth and twentieth centuries.

Under British rule, the missionary activities of other churches were restricted, and in 1922 the Roman Catholic religion was recognized in law as the religion of the country. A section of the Malta Criminal Code was passed, making it a criminal offense to criticize the Catholic religion in public. It is this long, uninterrupted, and unchallenged period of Catholic influence that is still felt today in Malta.

As late as the 1950s, the church dominated social life and determined the educational and social activities of the young in ways that are no longer acceptable in Western countries. The church ran its own schools, paid no taxes,

The Collegiate Church of Saint Paul in Rabat dates from the seventeenth century.

ROADSIDE SHRINES

Along the streets and roads in the Maltese islands, there are many small shrines to various saints. These Catholic roadside monuments are a European tradition dating back many centuries, and they are particularly common in rural areas. In olden times, they were wayside markers along routes of pilgrimage that helped religious travelers find their way.

Many still exist in predominantly Catholic European countries such as France, Italy, and Malta. Some shrines are simple, while others are quite elaborate. Many look like tiny chapels, and some are built into grottoes, or small rocky cavelike openings in a hillside. Many shrines feature a statue or painting of the Virgin Mary or a saint.

Passersby can stop at a shrine and offer a prayer as they proceed along their journey. In Catholicism, a person can pray to a certain saint to take a special interest in their problems. In Malta, shrines have padlocked contribution boxes known as niccec *(nee-chech), into which believers can deposit some money as they request saintly intercession. The proceeds go to the local church or a charity.*

and owned large tracts of land and property on the islands. Priests could not be prosecuted under Maltese law. The disputes of the 1950s and 1960s with the Labour Party postponed the inevitable decline of church power but could not prevent it.

Today, freedom of religion is enshrined in the constitution, but the country remains officially and predominantly Catholic. The islands of Malta form an archdiocese with more than 350 churches, two cathedrals, and an archbishop based in Valletta. Gozo has its own bishop.

ROMAN CATHOLICISM

Roman Catholicism is one of the three main branches of Christianity, the other two being Eastern Orthodoxy—the Orthodox Catholic Church—and

Saint Paul is of particular importance in Malta, and he is one of its three patron saints (the others being Agatha and Publius). Originally a Jew from Asia Minor (modern-day Turkey for the most part), the man who would become Saint Paul was born in 6 CE and trained as a rabbi. He was commonly known as Saul of Tarsus. In his early years, he actively persecuted the early disciples of

Jesus Christ in the area of Jerusalem, believing them to be a breakaway Jewish sect. But on a journey to Damascus, he had a vision of Christ telling him to become a missionary for Christianity. His life thereafter was a series of missionary journeys across Greece and as far as Malta, where he was shipwrecked en route to Rome. On his return from Malta, Saint Paul was arrested after riots by Jewish groups who opposed his preaching. He was executed in Rome in 62 CE.

The Church of Saint Paul in Rabat is said to be the first parish church on the islands. Near it is a grotto (shown above right) where the saint is believed to have spent most of his

time while on Malta. The walls of the grotto are believed to have miraculous curative properties. Beneath the church are catacombs (left) built into the soft limestone rock where tables have been carved into the rock for people to celebrate Christ's Last Supper.

According to folk tradition, there are no poisonous snakes in Malta today because Saint Paul removed all their venom after being bitten by one soon after he arrived.

A man sits outside the Basilica of the Blessed Virgin of Ta' Pinu on Gozo.

Protestantism. The Catholic Church traces its origins back to Jesus Christ and his Apostles, who were the founders of early Christendom. The Eastern and Roman branches of this church broke into two separate churches in 1054 CE. Protestantism didn't break from Roman Catholicism until the sixteenth century. Roman Catholics, like most Christians, believe in the Holy Trinity—the Father, the Son (Jesus Christ), and the Holy Spirit (or Holy Ghost)—as the three aspects of God. Each aspect is itself God, but there is only one God. In iconography, the Holy Spirit is often depicted as a flame or a white dove.

Unlike other forms of Christianity, Roman Catholicism recognizes the authority of the pope as the head of the church. He is said to be the successor to Saint Peter, the head of the Apostles. The pope resides and governs from Vatican City, an independent city-state within Rome. Although he is a mortal man, his decisions are understood to be informed by the Holy Spirit and are therefore considered infallible and in accordance with the essential doctrines of the church. This means that the various policies that are issued by the Vatican must be followed by all Catholics.

Roman Catholicism also emphasizes the adoration of the Virgin Mary. Small grottoes dedicated to the mother of Jesus Christ are maintained throughout the nation.

THE CHRISTIAN CALENDAR

In Malta the major Christian festivals are celebrated in traditional style. A Maltese tradition at Christmas is to give children shallow saucers of water in which are sown wheat seeds or other seeds. The seeds are kept in the dark until they sprout. They are then placed by the family's nativity scene, by the crib of the baby Jesus. This tradition may be a remnant of an earlier religion in which the harvest was significant.

In Valletta, an elaborate crèche scene is displayed in the main square at Christmastime.

Easter is traditionally celebrated with a procession on Good Friday. Penitents make the journey in as uncomfortable a way as they can. Young men are often hooded and wear white robes with heavy chains on their ankles. The belief is that the farther they can walk in such discomfort, the more of their sins will be forgiven.

Villages celebrate the feast day of their patron saint on the weekend nearest to the actual day. These feast days are very often the day of the year on which the saint died. Although these celebrations were once very religious events, most people today see them as secular occasions.

CELEBRATING PATRON SAINTS

Malta has three national patron saints, and in addition, each town and village has a patron saint of its own. Traditional festivals are primarily social occasions today, but they still retain a religious significance based on the worship of that saint. The pealing of church bells may be drowned out by the sound of exploding fireworks, but for devout Catholics, a visit to their church is the most important part of these festivities. Much effort and care goes into decorating the church inside and outside, and the climax of the event is a procession in which a life-sized statue of the patron saint is paraded through the streets.

Three days of prayer precede the festival. Every evening, singing takes place in the church, followed by a mass (Catholic church service) and a special service known as Benediction. Each village has its own hymn to its patron saint in a popular melody and an anthem set to operatic music. These evening services end with members of the congregation kissing the saint's relic, which is enshrined in an ornately decorated gold case.

White-robed men carry a statue of Jesus Christ during a Good Friday procession in the village of Luqa.

Colorful street decorations honor Saint Dominic on his feast day in Birgu.

On the eve of the feast day, another special service takes place in the church. When the mass is over, a hymn of praise, known as the Te Deum, from the first words of the Latin hymn, is sung. The life-sized statue of the saint rests overnight in the center of the nave, and bouquets of flowers are arranged around it as an act of homage. In the evening the holy relic is solemnly carried from a side chapel to the main altar.

On the evening of the feast day itself, the statue of the saint is carried shoulder-high out of the church and through the streets, while the relic of the saint is solemnly carried by a church dignitary. Monks and priests, dressed in their finest vestments, join the procession alongside lay members of devotional associations. These members wear their own colorful robes and walk behind their own huge banner displaying an emblem of their group.

SOME OTHER SAINTS

Just as each tiny village in Malta has its own saint, so does each profession. Some of the saints have particularly gruesome stories of martyrdom. Saint

Agatha fled to Malta from Italy in 249 CE, after refusing to marry the governor of Catania at the wish of Emperor Decius. In Malta, she is said to have spent her time in catacombs under the city, teaching and praying. When she left Malta and returned to Catania in 251, she was imprisoned and tortured before being burned to death. Her chapel is in Mdina.

Saint Luke is another sainted figure to have spent time on the island. He accompanied Paul on his journeys. A physician during his life, he is the patron saint of doctors, students, butchers, and artists. Saint Publius converted Malta to Christianity. He was made bishop of Malta and then Athens. Later martyred, he also was declared a saint.

Saint Agatha's Tower, also known as the Red Tower, is a large coastal watchtower in Mellieħa in the north of Malta. It was built between 1647 and 1649. Having fallen into disrepair, the tower was renovated in 2001 and is now open to the public.

ANCIENT RELIGIONS

The 5,500-year-old megalithic temples of Ġgantija ("Giants' tower") on the island of Gozo are believed to be the oldest freestanding monuments in the world, predating the pyramids. The remains of the temples suggest an Earth mother—worshipping civilization with complex religious ceremonies. Altars

LANGUAGE

An older man reads a newspaper on a bench in Valletta.

9

MALTESE AND ENGLISH ARE THE official languages of Malta. Most people can speak at least some English, but the Maltese language—even though it is spoken nowhere else in the world—is alive and well. Many Maltese can also speak, or at least understand, Italian; few citizens are monolingual.

Before the arrival of the British around 1800, the official language since 1530 had been Italian. In 1934, English and Maltese were declared the sole official languages. At that time, only about 15 percent of the population could speak English. Italian had been the primary language of government, commerce, education, and culture in Malta for more than eight hundred years.

TRACING THE ROOTS OF MALTESE

The Maltese language reveals the mixed history of the country, but the deep roots of the language are uncertain. It most likely developed from the Sicilian Arabic, a form of Arabic that developed in Sicily and Malta between the ninth and fourteenth centuries. Although that dialect was extinct in Sicily by the year 1300, it continued to be spoken in Malta and gradually evolved into present-day Maltese.

Another theory holds that the language might have its deepest roots in Carthaginian, or Punic, the language of Carthage—the ancient civilization of what is now the Mediterranean coast of Tunisia. If so, it would connect

Maltese, which is derived from an extinct Arabic dialect, is the only Semitic language (a family of languages which includes Arabic) serving as an official language of the European Union. Semitic languages are spoken across much of North Africa and the Middle East. Maltese is also the only Semitic language written in Latin, or Roman, script.

B YHEDA
LI
MIKIEL ANTON VASSALLI
1764-1829
MISSIER L-ILSIEN MALTI
INDIFEN F DAN IL-POST

B QIMA
DIN L ART HELWA
9 TA SETTEMBRU 1995

T OR NEAR THIS PLACE ARE THOUGHT
TO LIE THE REMAINS OF
MIKIEL ANTON VASSALLI 1764-1829
AND OF HIS WIDOW CATHERINE DE FREMEAUX
WHO WAS BURIED HERE IN 18[51]

This is the tombstone of the Maltese writer Mikiel Anton Vassalli (1764-1829), the "father of the Maltese Language."

Maltese to the Phoenician culture. One thing is certain, however. The arrival of the Arabs in 870 had a profound effect on the language, largely replacing the local tongue. In later centuries, the Sicilians (Normans) and then the Knights of Saint John followed. Sicilian, Latin, and Italian, which was later declared the country's official language, enjoyed high status for centuries—but the

*Here are some basic everyday expressions in Maltese. The first two words show a French influence and are pronounced very much like their French equivalents (*bonjour *and* bon soir*), while the word for "thank you" reveals the influence of Italian (*grazie*):*

Bonġu *(BON-joo)* . . . .*Good morning*
Bonswa *(BON-swah)* . . . .*Good evening*
Sahha *(sah-har)* . . . .*Good-bye*
Jekk joghgbok *(ye-hek YOJ-bok)* . . . .*Please*
Grazzi *(GRAHT-see)* . . . .*Thank you*
Iva *(EE-vah)* . . . .*Yes*
Le *(leh)* . . . .*No*
Titkellem bl-Ingliż? *(tit-kel-LEM Ling-LEEZE)* . . . . .*Do you speak English?*

Sicilian-Arabic dialect never died out. It was the common language of the working people. That tongue would become Maltese.

In 1800, when Malta became a British colony, the Maltese language began picking up English words and adding them to the mix. The historical source of modern Maltese vocabulary is 52 percent Italian/Sicilian; 20 percent English; with the remainder coming from Arabic, French, and Norman. Language is more than just vocabulary, however. The rules of grammar and pronunciation also play a large role in making a language what it is.

WRITTEN MALTESE

The first Maltese dictionaries were compiled in the seventeenth century. The earliest known prose writing in Maltese is a collection of religious sermons from 1739. The language of the sermons betrays a strong Italian influence in its choice of vocabulary, which is not surprising given that the church in Malta at that time was largely made up of Sicilians.

The current Maltese alphabet was introduced in 1924. Before then, various spelling systems were used, but the language has always been

The men who made up the Order of Saint John came from the aristocratic families of Europe, and their linguistic influence was felt in Malta over a period of 250 years. Like the Normans, they did not have much contact with the peasants of the islands. So although new words were constantly being added, the structure of the language spoken by ordinary people remained largely unchanged. The earliest examples of Maltese literature date back to the seventeenth century.

THE ITALIAN CONNECTION

The Maltese constitution was suspended by the British in the early 1930s, mainly as the result of a controversial attempt to promote Italian as the official language. The British claimed that only about 15 percent of the population spoke Italian. Italy's political leader, Benito Mussolini, on the other hand, claimed that the Maltese language was a dialect of Italian and that the Maltese people were Italian by race. There was, however, no linguistic basis to this claim, and the real nature of Mussolini's interest in Malta became clear when World War II broke out and Italian planes bombed the island.

ENGLISH IN MALTA

English was first introduced to Malta in the early nineteenth century when the British, then at war with France, took over the islands after the French garrison surrendered. At that time, the ruling class in Malta, including government officials and the Catholic Church, mostly spoke Italian, and little changed for a long time after the arrival of the British. English made little headway in Malta in the nineteenth century because the British exercised political power but

International newspapers are displayed at a stand in Valletta.

did not mix on a daily basis with ordinary people. In this way they were not very different from the Normans or the Knights of Saint John.

It was only in the twentieth century that English began to play an increasingly important role in the lives of the Maltese people. The replacement of Italian with English in the education system starting in the 1930s was pivotal because this affected ordinary young people and not just the educated elite. In the 1960s, Malta developed as a popular holiday destination for British tourists. An important reason for this, apart from the appealing climate of a Mediterranean island, was the perception that Malta was friendly toward the British. The long history of imperial rule had accustomed the Maltese to the habits of the British, and English was not an unfamiliar language. As tourism became increasingly important to the Maltese economy, and as English established itself as the world's international language, the Maltese became more and more willing to learn and use English.

Malta entered the twenty-first century as a bilingual society, where English and Maltese are used fluently as the means of communication, both officially and informally.

Travel guides in various languages are for sale in a shop in Valletta along Republic Street, or Triq Ir-Repubblika, as it's called in Maltese.

INTERNET LINKS

https://www.maltauncovered.com/culture/maltese-language-languages-spoken
This site provides an overview of the languages spoken in Malta, with popular phrases.

https://www.omniglot.com/writing/maltese.htm
Omniglot provides a good introduction to the Maltese language.

ARTS

Light shines through the oculus of the dome in the Rotunda of Mosta.

M ALTA'S HISTORY IS, TO SOME extent, written in its art. Of all the art forms, Malta's greatest claim to fame is that of its architecture. There are many superb examples of temples, churches, cathedrals, theaters, and palaces on the country's two small islands. Buildings spanning thousands of years speak to the extraordinary history of human creativity that occurred there in the middle of the Mediterranean world.

MEGALITHIC ART

Built between 3600 BCE and 2500 BCE, the stone temples of Malta are extraordinary examples of monumental ancient construction. Very little is known about the Neolithic (late Stone Age) societies that built those temples, and even less is known about why the society suddenly collapsed around 2500 BCE. Six of the sites, on both Malta and Gozo islands, are grouped together as a UNESCO World Heritage Site called the Megalithic Temples of Malta. The word "megalithic," which is derived from the ancient Greek words for "large" and "stone," is especially apt in describing Malta's temples because some of their stones weigh over 22 tons (20 metric tons). One megalith measures 23 by 10 feet (7 by 3 m).

10

Valletta was Europe's Capital of Culture 2018, an honor it shared that year with Leeuwarden-Fryslân in the Netherlands. This designation, bestowed by the European Union for one calendar year, allows the host city to sponsor a wide array of events and projects highlighting both local and international artistic expression.

LEISURE

A young man looks to sea on a bright day at Għarb, on Gozo.

11

LIFE IN MALTA IS GENERALLY pleasant and relaxed, which is why it attracts so many retired expats from other countries. The island nation's three hundred days of sunshine, on average, add to a leisurely frame of mind and pace of life. This is especially apparent in the refreshing practice of taking a casual stroll with a partner or a friend when the heat of the afternoon sun has subsided.

The Malta Marathon, first held in 1986, has become an established annual event for the Maltese as well as for hundreds of runners from around the world.

STROLLING IN THE STREET

This traditional feature of the Maltese lifestyle, that of dressing up in stylish clothes—but never overdressing—and going out for a social walk, helps define the difference between a Mediterranean culture as found in countries such as Malta and the more work-oriented, faster-paced lifestyle of Northern Europe.

Older people tend to walk in pairs, with their partner, relative, or friend, while younger people usually move in small groups. The activity provides an opportunity for informal conversation and a possible encounter with friends or neighbors who are also out walking. In towns, certain streets and routes, often the promenade that follows the course of the shoreline, are popular.

OTHER SPORTS

Water-based sports such as swimming, water polo, waterskiing, windsurfing, and sailing are also popular with the Maltese. Most of the country's land-based sports, apart from soccer, take place at Marsa. This large flat area was where the Turks set up base during the Great Siege of 1565. It is now the site of the country's major sports club, and it is where Malta's second most popular sport, horse racing, takes place.

Between October and May, weekly race meetings, including trotting races, are held. Trotting races—short and fast races using a pony (a smaller breed of horse), or even a donkey, harnessed to a small, compact vehicle called a sulky— are enormously popular, and many Maltese bet on them. Maltese teenagers prefer to spend their leisure time at the large ten-pin bowling alley and roller rink complex on the island of Malta.

A horse pulls a sulky on a racetrack in Marsa.

Fishing is popular with men, although it is enjoyed more as a form of relaxation than as an active sport. As a fishing license is not required, the activity is popular with casual fishermen. The rods used are unusually long because the best fish do not swim close to the shore. Enthusiasts have to clamber out onto the edges of rocky points to get as far out to the sea as possible.

Other sports enjoyed by the Maltese include horse riding, golf, tennis, squash, badminton, field hockey, basketball, polo, and archery. Golf dates back to 1888, when the game was introduced to Malta by the British governor. Polo is a stick-and-ball game played on horseback by two teams of four. Points are scored by hitting the ball with a handheld mallet into the opposing team's goal, and each game is divided into a series of seven-minute periods known as chukkers. The game has its origins in central Asia. The water-based version, water polo, was developed by the British in the nineteenth century and is played in swimming pools. Both sports were introduced into Malta by the British.

People fish off a rocky point in Valletta.

All countries have their own unique cultural traditions and idiosyncratic customs. Foreigners may find certain peculiar practices baffling or amusing, but most often they find them charming or even admirable. But there is a tradition in Malta that many people find disturbing. The European Union, in fact, finds it unacceptable. That's the Maltese craze for shooting birds.

The Maltese islands lie on the central flyway used by millions of birds each spring and fall as they migrate between Europe and Africa. Some 340 bird species use the islands as stopover points on their long migrations. Many of these species are endangered. A recent study showed that birds originating from a minimum of thirty-six European countries have been recorded migrating over Malta.

This should make Malta a bird-lover's paradise. But curiously, springtime finds the Maltese valleys echoing with the gunshots of up to ten thousand hunters. In Malta, this is spring hunting season, and the animal in the crosshairs is a bird—any bird. "If it flies, it dies," is the time-honored saying.

In spring and again in autumn, hunters—mostly men—gather in fields, public parks, and other places to shoot as many small birds as possible. Sparrows, finches, song birds, and up to one hundred thousand birds of prey, including more than thirty thousand kestrels, once became annual victims in the mass slaughters. Many ended up stuffed and displayed in trophy cabinets across Malta. And it was all not only legal but celebrated.

Maltese hunters parade in Rabat to celebrate the result of the hunting referendum on April 12, 2015.

But then along came the European Union. Once Malta had joined the economic, political, and increasingly environmental organization in 2003, it agreed to abide by its many rules. And the shooting of many of these protected birds is expressly forbidden by EU law under the Birds Directive. Nevertheless, the killing went on.

In 2008, the European Court of Justice ordered the Maltese government to stop the hunting and trapping of birds. However, Malta continued to allow the hunting of migratory turtle doves and quail for three weeks each spring. Springtime hunting is a particular concern to conservationists, because that is when the birds are nesting and raising young.

In 2015, Malta held a referendum on whether to continue spring hunting. Voter turnout was almost 75 percent, and by a small margin—50.44 to 49.56 percent—they voted to continue the spring bird hunt. The following year, ten thousand hunting licenses were issued in the small country.

By 2018, Malta had been forced to curtail the shooting of all but quail, at least officially. Hunters, however, paid little attention to the new law, according to activist observers, and some even deliberately targeted protected birds. Thousands of endangered turtle doves were illegally killed that season, along with birds of many other protected species. Those hunters claimed the activity was an ancient Maltese tradition, a part of their culture that they wished to preserve, and that they resented outside interference.

INTERNET LINKS

https://birdlifemalta.org/2018/04/rampant-killing-of-protected -birds-all-across-malta-and-gozo
This organization opposes the illegal hunting of birds in Malta.

https://www.financemalta.org/why-malta/malta-lifestyle
The attributes of life in Malta are presented on this financial services site.

https://www.welcome-center-malta.com/top-sports-in-malta -traditional-and-most-common
Soccer, boccie, horse racing, skeet shooting, and other sports are discussed on this page.

FESTIVALS

A burst of blue lights the sky during a
fireworks festival in Valletta.

12

MALTA IS A VERITABLE Mediterranean hotspot for festivals of all sorts. The calendar is crammed with celebrations and special events, from jazz to folk music to world music to theater, dance, and opera fests. Every village reveres its patron saint in high style, as is seen in the abundance of *festi* (FEST-e), or village feasts, that punctuate the social calendar between May and September.

The *festa* (FEST-a), or feast, has its origins in the religious traditions of village communities. The setting aside of at least one day each year to honor the village church's patron saint has become the occasion for each village and town to celebrate its own sense of communal identity.

FESTI

Preparing for a village festa is often a hectic activity because of the competition among neighboring villages to mount a more colorful and more exciting event. Festa events are scheduled well in advance and are meticulously planned to ensure that everything runs smoothly.

Celebrations take place over at least one weekend, and apart from the solemn church services and religious processions, there are numerous secular events that lend a nonreligious flavor to every festa. Indeed, for a growing number of Maltese, a visit to the church to appreciate the displays and ornamentation may be the only time in the year that they step inside their local church. The social and festive nature of the festa is reflected in the tremendous noise that accompanies such festivals, with every village announcing the imminent arrival of their festival by setting off fireworks.

The notion behind these pre-festa celebrations seems to be that the louder the noise, the more confidence the villagers have that their festa will be more glamorous than the previous year and more successful and popular than their neighboring village's event. Complementing the noise is the display of multicolored fireworks exploding across the sky. The drama is heightened by the thousands of small colored bulbs strung across streets and hung from public and private buildings.

A highlight of the festival is the processional march of a band, followed by a crowd of local people enjoying the atmosphere. The occasion is a unique blend

Confetti covers the street as folks enjoy the Mosta Festival in August, celebrating the Feast of the Assumption.

HISTORY OF THE FESTA

The origins of the festa go back to the sixteenth century, when the local nobility would play the part of the honorable patron. Once a year, the local landowner would finance a small celebration to gain the goodwill of the peasants. Over time, a sense of competition gradually developed between the landowners as some of them used the celebrations to display their generosity and power. Gifts of money to the local church were used to finance the purchase of a statue of the patron saint. The peasants themselves eventually joined in the planning and production of the festas.

By the early eighteenth century, a form of fireworks was used for the first time. A decisive factor in the development of the festival was the growing involvement of the Knights, as the Order of Saint John recognized the value of the celebrations in raising the morale of the poor. It was the wealth of the Knights that transformed these minor festivals into spectacular events. Then the British arrived on the scene with their military bands and pomp and ceremony. They encouraged villages to form their own bands because they, too, saw the value of helping the peasants forget their poverty for at least a few days.

Today, the organization and financing of village festivals is managed completely at the local level. There is no government subsidy. The rich still play a significant role in financing the celebrations and often donate lavish bouquets of flowers for decorating the statue of the patron saint.

of the formal and the informal because the musicians make impromptu stops along the way, pausing for complimentary refreshments. The climax takes place on Sunday when the statue of the patron saint is paraded through the streets, confetti is thrown from the windows of houses along the route, and fireworks light up the sky. At the end of the day, when the streets are empty, it can look like there has been a sudden downpour of colored snow because the pavements are literally carpeted in confetti.

Malta's fireworks displays are said to be among the finest to be seen anywhere in Europe. The Malta International Fireworks Festival is scheduled each year around the night of April 30 and May 1, partly to commemorate Malta's entrance into the European Union on May 1, 2004.

A girl in an elaborate costume parades down a street in Valletta during Carnival.

CARNIVAL

This was once a religious festival that preceded the first day of Lent, traditionally a period of fasting that leads up to Easter. The beginnings of this Maltese festival, however, date back to pre-Christian times. The festival has its origins in a pagan celebration to mark the end of winter, and the highlight of this week-long event is a procession of colorful floats that sets off just outside Valletta and makes its way through the gates of the city and into the capital. Some of the more artistic floats take the form of giant displays of flowers carefully laid out on the back of an open truck. Even more time-consuming to design and make are the striking costumes that appear in the parade.

Around the same time of the year, the island of Gozo holds a similar festive event, and although it is held on a much smaller scale, it shares with

Many of Malta's public holidays mark religious events. The few exceptions either celebrate nationalist events or commemorate workers' rights:

January 1	New Year's Day
February 10.	Saint Paul's Shipwreck
March 19	Saint Joseph's Day
March 31	Freedom Day
April	Good Friday, Easter weekend
May 1	Labor Day
June 7	Sette Giugno (commemoration of 1919 riot)
June 29	Feast of Saints Peter and Paul
August 15.	Feast of the Assumption
September 8	Great Siege of Victories (Our Lady of Victories)
September 21	Independence Day
December 8.	Feast of the Immaculate Conception
December 13	Republic Day
December 25	Christmas Day
December 26	Boxing Day

the Valletta festival historical roots based on a primitive celebration of the approach of spring.

MNARJA

The Feast of Saint Peter and Saint Paul on June 29 is a public holiday and the occasion for an important festival traditionally known as Mnarja (im-NAAR-ya), from a Maltese word meaning "light." Its origins are lost in time, but it may have been a country folk festival that has survived into modern times. This feast has always been considered a special day for everyone, particularly for the peasants who used to have their annual break at this time of year and tried to enjoy it to the fullest. The traditional start to the festival occurs some days before the event with a formal procession of Boy Scouts from the

A street decoration featuring the upside-down cross of Saint Peter is one of many that adorn the town of Nadur, on Gozo, for the Festival of Saint Peter and Saint Paul.

city of Mdina, accompanied by a band and members of the organizing committee, who carry and display the prizes that will later be awarded to winners of the horse races that will take place on June 29.

On the eve of the 29th, the festivities move to Buskett Gardens on the outskirts of Rabat, where an agricultural show is already bustling with activity. Some people will spend the night in the gardens, camping under the trees, and the sound of bands and Spanish guitars is heard until the early hours of the morning.

On the day of the 29th, attention switches back to Mdina, where traditional horse and donkey races take place. An amusing feature of these races is that the animals are ridden bareback, and the jockeys have to grip their mounts with their knees, while driving the animals forward with a short stick. In the seventeenth and eighteenth centuries, special races were held for slaves until they were abolished by Napoleon in 1798. After the races, the prizes are distributed, an ancient tradition that goes back at least three centuries, according to a Latin motto inscribed on the walls of the city: *Cuicumque legitime certaverit* ("For all who lawfully strive to win").

CHRISTMAS

Unlike the celebrations in many other European countries, Christmas in Malta is far less of a public festival and much less commercial in spirit. This is mainly because of the traditional religious significance that is still attached to Christmas. Familiar practices include the decorating of streets and buildings with colored lights and community groups singing carols in public places. Midnight mass is held at all Catholic churches, and nativity crèche scenes (*presepju*) are everywhere. Touring the various nativity displays is a popular activity. Another Christmas highlight, popular among children and adults alike, is the annual pantomime held at the Manoel Theater in Valletta, said to be the third-oldest working theater in Europe.

Christmas Day is essentially a family celebration. Families decorate Christmas trees and exchange gifts, but there is little of the shopping frenzy seen in some European and US cities in the weeks and days leading up to the holiday. Shops and businesses are all closed on December 25. One of the busiest places is the arrival hall of Malta's only international airport, as many Maltese working and living abroad return home to be with their families.

The Parish Church of Saint Peter's Chains in Birżebbuġa, Malta, glitters with Christmas decorations.

HOLY WEEK

Holy Week marks the religious celebrations leading up to Easter Sunday. As compared with most other festive occasions, it is a somber event, commemorating the death and resurrection of Jesus Christ. It starts on the

L-għanqud ta'
l-għeneb mill-
art imwegħda
simbol

Children reenact the Easter story in a Good Friday procession in Luqa.

Friday of the week before the Easter weekend with a major procession through the streets of Valletta and smaller processions in other towns.

On the following Thursday, traditional "Last Supper" displays are held in religious institutions in some towns, commemorating the last meal of Christ and his apostles, as described in the New Testament of the Bible. A traditional display features a table prepared for Christ and his twelve apostles with fresh loaves, wine jars, and pastries.

The next day is Good Friday, the day that traditionally marks the crucifixion of Christ. Good Friday is a public holiday, and all businesses and entertainment outlets are closed. Processions with life-sized statues depicting scenes associated with the biblical event take place in many towns.

Easter Sunday is a day of celebration, marking the Christian belief that on this day Christ was resurrected. Like Christmas Day, this is very much a

It would be difficult to imagine a Maltese festival that did not include the presence of a brass band. The bands' significance to the national culture has been recognized by the government, which plans to promote their popularity so that they do not die out like other cultural traditions. Band clubs have also been recognized as a useful way to encourage a love of music among the young.

*Malta has a large number of local bands, including a police band. The various bands claim some twenty-three thousand members (*bandisti*)—about 6.5 percent of the population! The oldest band clubs can trace their history back to the late nineteenth century. In 1999, the Saint Philip Band Club of Żebbuġ triumphantly announced that documents had been found proving their band had been founded in 1851.*

family occasion. Relatives and friends visit one another's houses, and Easter eggs are presented to children. A special sweet, the *figolla* (FIG-ole-ar), a pastry cut into various shapes such as the Maltese Cross, is prepared for this day. It is filled with marzipan and covered with colored icing.

INTERNET LINKS

https://www.maltafireworksfestival.com
This site features a short video of fireworks displays at the annual festival.

https://www.visitmalta.com/en/annual-festivals
This travel site lists Malta's annual festivals and special events.

FOOD

Patrons enjoy a fine November day at an outdoor café in the village of Victoria on Gozo.

13

JUST AS MALTA LIES RIGHT IN THE middle of the Mediterranean Sea, its cuisine reflects a lively mix of Mediterranean cookery. Sicilian, Provençal, Spanish, and North African tastes combine with a strong British influence, reflecting the country's history. Obvious examples of this are pasta, introduced from Italy, and British fare such as fish and chips. The first appearance of British food may have its origins in colonial history, but the annual invasion by hundreds of thousands of vacationers from Britain has helped popularize some of these dishes in restaurants and, indirectly, in the homes of Maltese families.

Many of the more fashionable restaurants in Malta today are influenced by Italian or French cuisine. However, Malta also has a distinctive Maltese cuisine that, like its language, has managed to survive and prosper, despite centuries of foreign domination.

Although tourists to Malta are sometimes shocked, horse meat is just another traditional dish found on restaurant menus, along with quail and rabbit.

Customers shop for fresh fruits and vegetables at an outdoor market in Marsaxlokk.

RURAL FARE

The Maltese diet is the product of a rural society, but the country's climate and ecology has also made a significant contribution. Many vegetables can be grown throughout the year and are readily available to all families. The scarcity of firewood for ovens in the days when electricity or gas was not commonly available accounts for the tradition of cooking food slowly in earthenware pots.

In the past, it was not unusual to take food to the village baker to be roasted in his oven after the bread had been taken out for the day. Although modern technology has eliminated the need to do this, this style of cooking continues to influence the nature and taste of traditional dishes. Even the tradition of taking food to the baker has not died out completely—on Sundays this can still be observed in some villages in Gozo.

SOUPS

A rustic lifestyle accounts for the popularity of soups in Malta. Because the vegetables are grown locally, a glut of some types of vegetables occurs now and then. This reduces their price and encourages people to combine their flavors over slow cooking. *Minestra* (MIN-ess-traa), a type of minestrone, is often prepared for lunch or as a first course for an evening meal, but it can easily be a filling meal in itself.

A hearty bowl of *aljotta* features giant shrimp, clams, mussels, fish, and calamari.

Another vegetable dish is *soppa tal-armla* (SOP-pah taal AM-laa), or widow's soup, which typically uses white and green vegetables and is traditionally served with chunks of goat cheese in the broth. *Kusksu* (kus-KSUE), is a vegetable soup with broad beans and tiny couscous-like pasta. This, too, is served with chunks of Maltese cheese in the bowl. *Aljotta* (AL-yacht-ta), a garlicky fish soup or stew, is a Maltese take on bouillabaisse, the French Provençal favorite. It's especially popular in the summer months, when fish is plentiful. In the winter, *kawlata* is a warming cabbage and pork soup.

NATIONAL DISHES

Fenek (fe-NECK), or rabbit, is one of Malta's most popular and distinctive dishes. It is eaten stewed, roasted, or fried. The origins of this dish are not difficult to understand, for when families were poor and food was scarce, it was always possible to hunt or trap a rabbit. Nowadays, wild rabbits may no longer be abundant in the countryside, but the popularity of rabbit as a dish has not diminished, and rabbits are reared especially for the kitchen.

Another national dish is *lampuka* (lam-POO-ka), which is a seasonal fish called mahi-mahi or dorado. The fish is relatively easy for local fishermen to catch with nets. The fish is fried or baked in a pie with olives, cauliflower, spinach, chestnuts, and raisins. Almost as popular is *bragioli* (BRA-geo-lee), tiny parcels of stuffing wrapped in slices of beef and cooked slowly at low temperature.

Malta's favorite cheese is *ġbejna* (j-BAY-nah). These small white rounds are made on small family farms on Gozo from sheep's or goat's milk. Each little cheese is shaped in a 3-inch (7.6 cm) *qwieleb*, or cheese basket.

BREAD

Sourdough Maltese bread is baked on the surface of an oven that gives it a firm crust but a soft, light center. The customary way to eat the bread is by adding olive oil, hence its name *ħobż biż-żejt* (hops BIZ-zeyt), which translates simply as "bread with oil." Tomatoes are first rubbed onto a slice of the bread, coloring it naturally. Peppers and capers are then added, before finally pouring on the olive oil.

Ftira (FEER-tee-rah) is a low-rise, ring-shaped, small, less-crusty Maltese bread that is usually baked in a very hot oven. In Gozo, ftira filled with sardines or anchovies is a typical supper snack during Lent fast days, when eating meat is not allowed.

A display of traditional Maltese breads entices hungry shoppers.

Eating rabbit in Malta was once a revolutionary act. The Knights of Malta prohibited the islanders from eating rabbit, except when the Feast of Saints Peter and Paul was held at

the end of June. Eating fenek, *therefore was a way of resisting their rule. At least that's one theory for the popularity of rabbit today in Maltese cuisine*

    Stuffat tal-fenek, *or rabbit stew, is often called the national dish. The meat is lightly browned with garlic and herbs, then simmered for several hours, ideally in a terra-cotta casserole,*

in a rich red wine tomato sauce with potatoes and carrots. Crusty bread soaks up the rich sauce. Traditionally, rabbit stew is served on spaghetti and is then called fenkata. *It's a favorite on the feast day of Saint Peter and Saint Paul to this day!*

PASTA

Maltese families do not eat pasta as frequently as Italians do, but the dish is enormously popular, both in the home and in restaurants. Two of the most popular traditional dishes are baked pasta—*timpana* (TIM-paa-nah) and *mqarrun fil-forn* (IM-ah-roon ill-fourn). Both dishes are made of macaroni with layers of meat, cheese, tomatoes, and eggs, and timpana is wrapped in light pastry.

A dish of *timpana*

DESSERTS

The Maltese love sweets, and there are many bakeries in the towns selling cookies and pastries. There are a number of traditional Maltese desserts.

TRADITIONAL MALTESE COCONUT PISTACCOS

TRADIIIDNAL mALTESE CANNOLI

Maltese sweets are displayed in a bakery window.

Nougat and hot, date-stuffed fried fritters are popular. Another favorite, usually eaten at the end of a meal with tea or coffee, is *kannoli* (can-OH-lee), a tube-shaped confection of deep-fried crisp pastry filled with a mixture of fresh-whipped cream, small pieces of candied fruit and chocolate, and ricotta cheese. A light dusting of powdered sugar and pistachios completes this delicacy, which originated in Sicily.

DRINKS

The Phoenicians may have first brought the skill of making wine to Malta. The process was then revived in the seventeenth century by the Knights of Saint John. Today, local grapes are used to produce wines that carry floral and fruity flavors. The strongest wines are produced on Gozo by small family enterprises.

The Maltese are not heavy beer drinkers, although there is a popular local beer called Cisk. There's also a popular non-alcoholic drink called Kinnie, which is made using herbs for a distinctive, bittersweet taste. Malta also produces a liquor called *bajtra* (BITE-trah) from the fruit of the prickly-pear cactus. It has a bright pink color and a sweet taste.

A can of Kinnie sits on a wall at a historic mansion in Paceville, Malta.

INTERNET LINKS

http://www.ilovefood.com.mt/maltese-cuisine
This Maltese site lists many recipes.

https://www.maltauncovered.com/culture/maltese-food
This site describes many favorite Maltese dishes and provides links to recipes.

http://old.culturemalta.org/62/Maltese-Cuisine
This Maltese culture site gives an overview of the country's cuisine and several recipes.

SOPPA TAL-ARMLA (WIDOW'S SOUP)

It's traditional to put a round of ġbejna in this soup, but the cheese is unavailable in the United States and there's no other cheese exactly like it. Substitute with ricotta salata, a mild feta, or another creamy or crumbly white goat or sheep's cheese. Some people poach eggs in the soup.

2 tablespoons butter or olive oil, or
  a combination
1 medium onion, peeled and sliced
3—4 cloves garlic, finely chopped
1 Tbsp tomato paste
2 carrots, peeled and sliced
1 stick celery, sliced
½ small cauliflower, broken into
  small florets
1 small kohlrabi, chopped (optional)
2 potatoes, peeled and diced
1 cup green peas
1 cup broad beans (fava beans, or substitute edamame, lima beans, or butter beans)
Chicken broth or vegetable broth
Salt and pepper, to taste
6 eggs, optional

In a large soup pot, sauté the onion in the oil and butter. Add the garlic and sauté lightly. Stir in the tomato paste.

Add all of the vegetables and enough broth or stock to cover. Add the seasonings. Bring to a boil, cover, and lower the heat.

Simmer for about 30 minutes or until vegetables are cooked.

If using the eggs, carefully break eggs into the soup. Add chunks of cheese and push down into the broth. Cover and cook another 5—10 minutes or until the eggs are cooked and the cheese is lightly melted. Serve hot.

ĦOBŻ BIŻ-ŻEJT (BREAD WITH OIL)

This open sandwich is much more than its name implies.

4 tablespoons olive oil
4 large, thick slices crusty bread
2 large ripe tomatoes, sliced in half
2 ounces crumbled ġbejniet (substitute feta)
1 5-ounce can tuna in olive oil, drained
2 Tbsp capers, drained
2 Tbsp chopped olives
Ground black pepper, to taste

In a large, flat-bottomed dish, dip one side of each bread slice in olive oil. Carefully transfer bread slices to a plate. Rub tomato halves onto bread slices, leaving plenty of pulp, then discard tomatoes.

Top each bread slice with one quarter of the cheese, tuna, olives, and capers. Sprinkle with pepper.

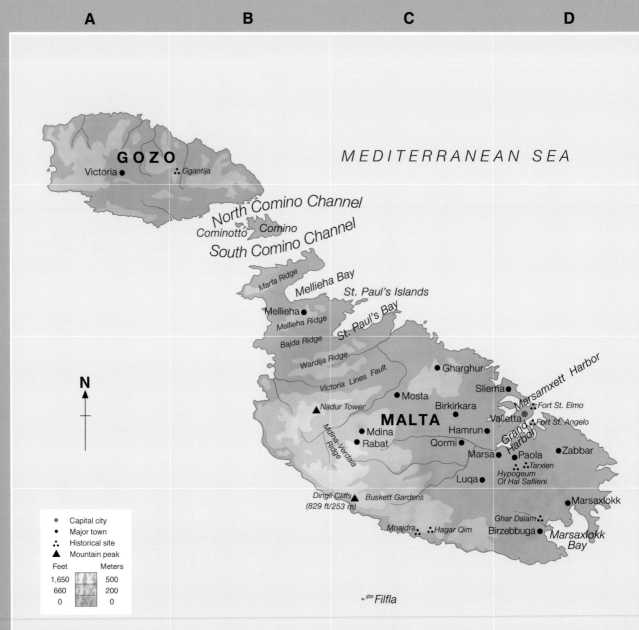

A **B** **C** **D**

1

2

3

4

GOZO

Victoria ●   ∴ Ggantija

MEDITERRANEAN SEA

North Comino Channel

Cominotto   *Comino*

South Comino Channel

Marfa Ridge

Mellieha Bay

St. Paul's Islands

Mellieha ●

Mellieha Ridge

St. Paul's Bay

Bajda Ridge

Wardija Ridge

● Gharghur

Victoria Lines Fault

Sliema ●

Marsamxett Harbor

N

▲ Nadur Tower

● Mosta

Birkirkara ●

MALTA

Valletta
∴ Fort St. Elmo

Fort St. Angelo

● Mdina

● Rabat

Mdina-Verdala Ridge

Hamrun ●

Qormi ●

Marsa ●

Grand Harbor

Paola ●

● Zabbar

∴ Tarxien

Hypogeum Of Hal Saflieni

Luqa ●

Dingli Cliffs ▲ *Buskett Gardens*
(829 ft/253 m)

Ghar Dalam ∴

● Marsaxlokk

Mnajdra ∴   ∴ *Hagar Qim*

Birzebbuga ●

Marsaxlokk Bay

● Capital city
● Major town
∴ Historical site
▲ Mountain peak

Feet		Meters
1,650		500
660		200
0		0

Filfla

MAP OF MALTA

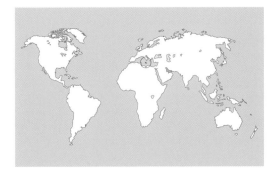

ECONOMIC MALTA

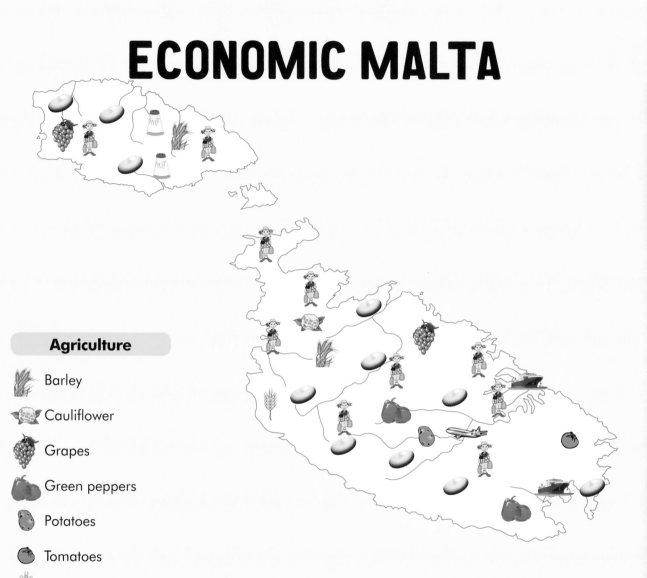

Agriculture

- 🌾 Barley
- 🥬 Cauliflower
- 🍇 Grapes
- 🫑 Green peppers
- 🥔 Potatoes
- 🍅 Tomatoes
- 🌾 Wheat

Services

- ✈️ Airport
- 🚢 Port
- 🧳 Tourism

Natural Resources

- 🪨 Limestone
- 🧂 Salt

ABOUT THE ECONOMY

(all statistics are estimates)

GROSS DOMESTIC PRODUCT (OFFICIAL EXCHANGE RATE)
$12.58 billion (2017)

GDP GROWTH
6.7 percent (2017)

GDP COMPOSITION, BY SECTOR OF ORIGIN
Agriculture: 1.1 percent
Industry: 10.2 percent
Services: 88.7 percent (2017)

CURRENCY
Euro (€)
US$1 = €0.89 (December 2018)

WORKFORCE
206,300 (2017)

WORKFORCE BY OCCUPATION
Agriculture: 77.7 percent
Industry: 20.7 percent
Services: 77.7 percent (2016)

UNEMPLOYMENT RATE
4.6 percent (2017)

POPULATION BELOW POVERTY LINE
16.3 percent (2015)

INFLATION
1.3 percent (2017)

AGRICULTURAL PRODUCTS
Potatoes, cauliflower, grapes, wheat, barley, tomatoes, citrus, cut flowers, green peppers, pork, milk, poultry, and eggs

MAJOR EXPORTS
Machinery and transportation equipment, mineral fuels and petroleum products, manufactured and semi-manufactured goods

MAJOR IMPORTS
Mineral fuels, oils and oil products, machinery and transport equipment, manufactured and semi-manufactured goods

MAIN TRADE PARTNERS
Italy, Germany, France, United Kingdom

CULTURAL MALTA

Ġgantija
Ġgantija is a Neolithic-age megalithic temple complex on Gozo. The Ġgantija temples are the earliest of a series of megalithic temples in Malta. Together with other similar structures, the Megalithic Temples of Malta have been designated a UNESCO World Heritage Site.

Manoel Theater
The Manoel Theater is reputed to be Europe's third-oldest working theater, and the oldest working theater in the Commonwealth of Nations. Located on Old Theater Street in Valletta, it is now Malta's National Theater and home to the Manoel Theater Museum.

The Mosta Dome
The Mosta Dome is a church in Mosta. It has the third-largest church dome in Europe and the ninth-largest in the world, with a diameter of 122 feet (37 m). It was designed by the Maltese architect Giorgio Grognet.

National Museum of Archaeology
The National Museum of Archaeology in Valletta displays an exceptional array of artifacts from Malta's unique prehistoric periods, starting with the arrival of humans in the Ghar Dalam phase (5200 BCE) and running up to the Tarxien phase (2500 BCE).

Ramla Bay
Situated on the tranquil isle of Gozo, this is an excellent unspoiled beach set in a beautiful valley. The color of the sand has given this beach its name, Ramla (il-Hamra), which literally means "red beach."

Saint John's Co-cathedral and Museum
Saint John's Co-cathedral and Museum was built as the temple of the Knights of Saint John. It is home to an impressive collection of art and artifacts, and is an important shrine and a sacred place of worship.

Saint Paul's Cathedral
Saint Paul's Cathedral is built on the site where governor Publius was reported to have met Saint Paul after his shipwreck off the Maltese coast. The cathedral has a substantial collection of silver plates and coins, and some carvings by the German artist Albrecht Dürer.

Mdina
Mdina, the old capital of Malta, is a medieval walled town situated on a hill in the center of the island. Much of its present architecture reflects the time of the Arab rulers of Malta until the Norman conquest in 1091 CE.

Catacombs of Saint Paul and Saint Agatha
These catacombs in the town of Rabat were used in Roman times to bury the dead because, according to Roman culture, it was unclean to bury the dead in the city. Catacombs were also where early Christians secretly met for worship.

Hypogeum
The Hypogeum in Paola, Malta, is a subterranean structure that was used as a necropolis in prehistoric times. Thought to have originally been a sanctuary, it is the only prehistoric underground temple in the world. It became a UNESCO World Heritage Site in 1980.

Saluting Battery, Upper Barracca Gardens
The battery is part of Valletta's old fortifications and provides gun salutes on national and religious festivals. It also used to mark time by firing at sunrise, midday, and sunset. There is a gorgeous view of Malta and the Grand Harbour from the battery.

Tarxien Temples
The Tarxien Temples are an archaeological complex in Tarxien, Malta. They date back to approximately 2800 BCE. Of particular interest at the temple site is the rich and intricate stonework, which includes depictions of domestic animals carved in altars.

ABOUT THE CULTURE

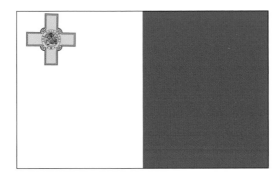

(all statistics are estimates)

OFFICIAL NAME
Republic of Malta

LAND AREA
122 square miles (316 square km)

CAPITAL
Valletta

MAJOR TOWNS
Birkirkara, Qormi, Mosta, Zabbar, Sliema

MAJOR ISLANDS
Malta, Gozo, Comino

HIGHEST POINT
Dingli Cliffs (829 feet/253 m)

POPULATION
449,043 (2018)

ETHNIC GROUPS
Maltese (the descendants of ancient Carthaginians and Phoenicians with strong elements of Italian and other Mediterranean stock)

RELIGIONS
Roman Catholicism: 98 percent
Others: 2 percent

MAIN LANGUAGES
Maltese (official), English (official),

LIFE EXPECTANCY
Total population: 82.7 years
Male: 80.6 years
Female: 84.8 years (2018)

BIRTHRATE
10 births per 1,000 population (2018)

DEATH RATE
7.9 deaths per 1,000 population (2018)

INFANT MORTALITY RATE
4.7 deaths per 1,000 live births (2018)

LITERACY
94.4 percent (2015)

TIMELINE

IN MALTA	IN THE WORLD

720 BCE
A Greek colony is founded on Malta.

753 BCE
Rome is founded.

80 BCE
The islands come under the control of Carthage, a former Phoenician colony, and rapidly develop into a Carthaginian naval base.

218 BCE
Invasion of Malta by the Roman Empire

41 CE
The Maltese are granted municipal privileges by Rome.

600 CE
Height of the Mayan civilization

870
Malta is conquered by Arabs, who introduce improved agricultural and irrigation systems.

1000
The Chinese perfect gunpowder and begin to use it in warfare.

1091
Norman rule is established over Malta.

1530
Emperor Charles V grants the Maltese islands to the Knights of Saint John.

1530
Beginning of transatlantic slave trade organized by the Portuguese in Africa

1798
Napoleon seizes the islands from the Knights.

1799
Britain takes Malta under its protection.

1814
Malta becomes a Crown colony of the British Empire.

1869
The Suez Canal is opened.

1914
World War I begins.

1934
English and Maltese are declared the official languages of Malta; Italian is excluded.

1939
World War II begins.

1942
King George VI awards the Malta the George Cross—Britain's highest civilian decoration—for heroism during World War II.

1945
The United States drops atomic bombs on Hiroshima and Nagasaki, Japan. World War II ends.

1947
Self-government granted.

1959
Self-government revoked.

IN MALTA	IN THE WORLD
1962	
Self-government restored.	
1964	
Full independence granted.	**1969**
1971	US astronaut Neil Armstrong becomes
Dom Mintoff's Malta Labour Party takes power.	first person to walk on the moon.
1974	
Malta becomes a republic.	
1984	
Mintoff resigns, succeeded by	**1986**
Carmelo Mifsud-Bonnici.	Nuclear power disaster at Chernobyl in Ukraine.
	1991
1995	Breakup of the Soviet Union.
Malta joins NATO's Partnership for	**1997**
Peace program, only to leave in 1996.	Hong Kong is returned to China.
2001	**2001**
Pope John Paul II visits Malta and beatifies	Al-Qaeda terrorists stage 9/11 attacks in New
three Maltese clerics at an open-air ceremony.	York, Washington, DC, and Pennsylvania.
	2003
2004	War in Iraq begins.
Malta is one of ten new countries to join the EU.	
2008	**2008**
Malta adopts the euro.	US elects first African American
	president, Barack Obama.
	2009
2011	Outbreak of H1N1 flu around the world.
Maltese parliament passes a law allowing divorce.	
2013	
Joseph Muscat becomes the	**2015–2016**
prime minister of Malta.	ISIS launches terror attacks in Belgium and France.
2017	**2017**
Azure Window collapses in heavy storms.	Donald Trump becomes US president.
Reporter Daphne Caruana	Hurricanes devastate Houston, Caribbean
Galizia is killed by a car bomb.	islands, and Puerto Rico.
2018	**2018**
Valletta serves for one year as	Winter Olympics in South Korea.
Europe's Capital of Culture.	
2019	**2019**
Times of Malta launches anti-hate campaign.	Anti-government protests in Venezuela and France.

GLOSSARY

auberge
An inn of residence for the Knights of the Order of Saint John.

catacomb
An underground cemetery.

eurozone
A currency union of European Union member states that have adopted the euro as their sole legal tender.

figolla (FIG-ole-ar)
A pastry cut into various shapes, such as the Maltese Cross, prepared for Easter Sunday celebrations.

ghana (ANN-aa)
Poems that are sung to musical accompaniment.

gregale (grey-GAH-lay)
A cooling wind that blows in from the mountains in Italy.

ħobż biż-żejt (hops BIZ-zeyt)
Maltese bread with olive oil.

kannoli (can-OH-lee)
A tube-shaped dessert of deep-fried crisp pastry with a creamy ricotta-based filling.

karozzin (ca-rotts-SEEN)
Horse-drawn carriage.

kusksu (kus-KSUE)
A traditional vegetable soup made from broad beans with pasta and tomatoes.

luzzijiet (LUT-tsie-yiet)
Traditional Maltese fishing boats.

megalithic
Structures made of large stones, utilizing an interlocking system without the use of mortar or cement.

mqarrun fil-forn (IM-ah-roon ill-fourn)
A traditional pasta-based dish.

necropolis
A prehistoric burial ground.

niccec (nee-chech)
Contribution boxes placed at shrines to the saints.

scree
A steep mass of broken rock on the side of a mountain.

sirocco
A warm and sultry wind that blows across Malta from the Sahara at the beginning and end of each summer.

Te Deum
A hymn of praise sung at a special service on the eve of a feast day.

FOR FURTHER INFORMATION

BOOKS

DK Eyewitness Travel. *Top 10: Malta & Gozo*. London, UK: Dorling Kindersley Limited, 2015.

Rix, Juliet. *Malta and Gozo*. Bradt Country Guides. Chalfont St. Peter, UK: Bradt Travel Guides, 2016.

ONLINE

CIA World Factbook: Malta. https://www.cia.gov/library/publications/the-world-factbook/geos/mt.html

Government of Malta. https://www.gov.mt/en

The *Guardian*: Malta Archives. https://www.theguardian.com/world/malta

Heritage Malta. http://heritagemalta.org

Lonely Planet. https://www.lonelyplanet.com/malta

Malta Independent. http://www.independent.com.mt

Malta Today. https://www.maltatoday.com.mt

Malta Tourism Authority. http://www.mta.com.mt

Times of Malta. https://www.timesofmalta.com

MUSIC

Folk Songs and Music From Malta. Folkways Records, 2012

Treasures from Baroque Malta. Rose Records, 2017

Historic Organs of Malta and Gozo. Priory/Allegro, 2014.

BIBLIOGRAPHY

BirdLife Malta. "Rampant Killing of Protected Birds All Across Malta and Gozo, Thousands of Turtle Doves Believed Shot Despite Season Supposedly Open Only for Quail." April 19, 2018. https://birdlifemalta.org/2018/04/rampant-killing-of-protected-birds-all-across-malta-and-gozo.

Costa, Massimo. "Manufacturing Now Second Most Important Employer in Malta." *Malta Today*, January 15, 2018. https://www.maltatoday.com.mt/news/national/83716/manufacturing_now_second_most_important_employer_in_malta#.XC-h_1xKjcs.

Encyclopaedia Britannica. "Malta." https://www.britannica.com/place/Malta.

Engel, Matthew. "Malta: An Island of Secrets and Lies." *New Statesman America*, February 27, 2018. https://www.newstatesman.com/world/europe/2018/02/malta-island-secrets-and-lies.

European Union. "Malta." https://europa.eu/european-union/about-eu/countries/member-countries/malta_en.

Garrett, Bradley L. "Malta's Secret Tunnels: Inside the Newly Discovered Underworld of Valletta." *Guardian*, February 20, 2017. https://www.theguardian.com/cities/2017/feb/20/malta-secret-tunnels-inside-newly-discovered-underworld-valletta.

Heritage Malta. http://heritagemalta.org.

Independent. "EU Commission Details Malta's Environmental Challenges and Opportunities." February 12, 2017. http://www.independent.com.mt/articles/2017-02-12/local-news/EU-Commission-details-Malta-s-environmental-challenges-and-opportunities-6736170267.

Kennedy, Merrit. "Malta's Landmark 'Azure Window' Rock Formation Collapses." National Public Radio, March 8, 2017. https://www.npr.org/sections/thetwo-way/2017/03/08/519273713/maltas-landmark-azure-window-rock-formation-collapses.

Kulish, Nicholas. "In Journalist's Murder, a Test for Malta, and the European Union." *New York Times*, April 17, 2018. https://www.nytimes.com/2018/04/17/world/europe/journalist-murder-malta-eu.html.

Malta, Government of. https://www.gov.mt/en.

Malta Today. https://www.maltatoday.com.mt.

Malta Tourism Authority. "Tourism in Malta: Fact and Figures 2017." http://www.mta.com.mt.

McCormick, Mark. "'If It Flies, It Dies': The Tradition of Bird Hunting in Malta and How You Can Help End the Brutality." *One Green Planet,* 2014. https://www.onegreenplanet.org/animalsandnature/the-tradition-of-bird-hunting-in-malta.

Reel, Monte. "Why the EU Is Furious With Malta." *Bloomberg Businessweek*, September 11, 2018. https://www.bloomberg.com/news/features/2018-09-11/why-the-eu-is-furious-with-malta.

Reporters Without Borders. "Murder at the Heart of the EU." https://rsf.org/en/malta.

Timeanddate.com. "Holidays in Malta 2019." https://www.timeanddate.com/holidays/malta/2019.

US Department of State. "US Relations With Malta." https://www.state.gov/r/pa/ei/bgn/5382.htm.

INDEX

INDEX